65/Net

English Language Workshop

Vocabulary Building 2

Workbook

Betty Kirkpatrick MA

Learners Publishing

First published 2001 by **Learners Publishing Pte Ltd**
222 Tagore Lane, #03-01 TG Building, Singapore 787603

Reprinted 2002 (twice), 2003

Email: learnpub@learners.com.sg
Visit our website: http://www.learners.com.sg

ISBN 981 4070 29 7

Printed by Seng Lee Press Pte Ltd, Singapore

ASSOCIATE COMPANIES

R I C-Learners International Limited
P.O. Box 332
Greenwood
Western Australia 6924

R I C Publications Limited (Asia)
5th floor, Gotanda Mikado Building
2-5-8 Hiratsuka
Shinagawa-ku Tokyo
JAPAN 142-0051
Tel: 03 3788 9201
Fax: 03 3788 9202
Email: elt@ricpublications.com
Website: www.ricpublications.com

Preface

The purpose of this *Vocabulary Building Workbook Series* is to provide students with practice on vocabulary development. The use of passages, rather than a single example sentence of the kind found in most dictionaries, demonstrates in a lively and graphic way just how words and sentences relate to each other and how English is actually put together.

Because English has many words that have several meanings, it is very easy to use the same word several times in a piece of writing or speech. Some of these words, such as the adjectives **nice**, **good** and **great**, are rather vague and imprecise in some of their meanings and it is, therefore, particularly common to overuse them.

Other words, such as the verbs **cover** and **touch**, may not have this problem of imprecision but they still have so many meanings that it is tempting to use them too frequently. The words themselves are perfectly acceptable in their various contexts. It is their overuse which should be avoided.

If you want to make your English speech and writing more interesting, it is important to try to introduce some variety by extending the scope of your vocabulary. This book will assist you in achieving this aim, as well as helping you to avoid repetition, by suggesting words which are similar in meaning to the word which you first thought of. Such words are known as synonyms.

Each unit of this text includes:

- a specially written passage containing the same key word used ten times with different meanings, sometimes including informal meanings;
- a list of synonyms for each meaning, together with guidance on context or examples of usage;
- the same passage with blanks for students to fill in the appropriate synonyms of the key word; and
- a set of questions to test how much knowledge students have gained from the passage and list of synonyms.

Contents

1

Postponed Celebrations

Read the following passage carefully, paying particular attention to the words in bold type.

'I'm feeling absolutely **dead**!' said Lucy. She and her fellow-students had just finished sitting six exams in the course of three days. In vain, they had asked the head teacher for more time between the exams, but he was **dead** to anything that interfered with the smooth running of the school. Changes to the exam schedule had been raised in previous years and were now, as far as he was concerned, a **dead** issue. The previous head teacher had been more inclined to listen to the students, but he had been **dead** for two years. Now the students were trying to recover from exams which had been very difficult. Although they were usually very talkative, today there was a **dead** silence in the room. Julie, who was usually extremely lively, was sitting looking out of the window with **dead** eyes. Then Mike started complaining that his fingers had gone **dead** because of all the writing. Bert had tried to phone his parents, but it was **dead.** Apparently, there was a fault on the line. All their plans to go out and celebrate the end of the exams seemed to have come to a **dead** halt. In any case, as Phil pointed out, the town was always **dead** on Wednesday nights. They all decided that, instead of going out, they would all prefer to get some sleep. They would postpone their celebrations until the weekend when they would be less tired.

Know the Meaning

dead *adjective*

1 *(informal) (of a person: I feel dead after that long walk.)* **exhausted, worn out, tired out, tired.**

2 *(of a person: Jim's parents were dead to his pleas for more money.)* **unresponsive, indifferent, unmoved by, unsympathetic.**

3 *(of a subject, issue, etc: The subject is dead—no one wants to discuss it any more.)* **outdated, outmoded, past.**

4 *(of a person: Meg's father has been dead for two years.)* **deceased, gone, late** *(when coming before the noun: Meg's late father.)*

5 *(It was a dead certainty that Mark would win.)* **complete, utter, absolute.**

6 *(of an expression, eyes, etc: Jackie sat there with a dead look on her face.)* **expressionless, emotionless, blank, empty.**

7 *(of a part of the body: I was kneeling down and my foot went dead.)* **numb,** (be) **without feeling.**

8 *(of a phone or phone line: The phone is dead—I must report the fault.)* **not working, inoperative, off.**

9 *(The train came to a dead halt.)* **abrupt, sudden.**

10 *(of a place: Bill complained that the seaside resort was dead in the winter.)* **dull, boring, uneventful, inactive.**

Exercise 1

Find a suitable word that is similar in meaning to 'dead' for each blank.

'I'm feeling absolutely **1.** ____yes____ !' said Lucy. She and her fellow-students had just finished sitting six exams in the course of three days. In vain, they had asked the head teacher for more time between the exams, but he was **2.** ____________ to anything that interfered with the smooth running of the school. Changes to the exam schedule had been raised in previous years and were now, as far as he was concerned, a **3.** ____________ issue. The previous head teacher had been more inclined to listen to the students, but he had been **4.** ____________ for two years. Now the students were trying to recover from exams which had been very difficult. Although they were usually very talkative, today there was a **5.** ____________ silence in the room. Julie, who was usually extremely lively, was sitting looking out of the window with **6.** ____________ eyes. Then Mike started complaining that his fingers had gone **7.** ____________ because of all the writing. Bert had tried to phone his parents, but it was **8.** ____________ . Apparently, there was a fault on the line. All their plans to go out and celebrate the end of the exams seemed to have come to a **9.** ____________ halt. In any case, as Phil pointed out, the town was always **10.** ____________ on Wednesday nights. They all decided that, instead of going out, they would all prefer to get some sleep. They would postpone their celebrations until the weekend when they would be less tired.

Exercise 2

Rewrite the following sentences, replacing the words in bold with a suitable alternative.

1 Peter said that it was a **dead** certainty that Jack would be late.

2 I've been carrying a heavy bag and my fingers have gone **dead**.

3 The waitress was feeling **dead** after her long shift.

4 We thought the phone was working again–– but it's still **dead**.

5 The teacher was **dead** to the children's request for more time to play.

6 The car came to a **dead** stop and wouldn't start again.

7 Parliament has voted against the bill and so the subject is **dead** now.

8 Phil said that the village was **dead** and that he wanted to live in the city.

9 Matt's brother has been **dead** for about a year.

10 Jane is suffering from depression and has a **dead** expression.

2 A Trio of Friends

Know the Meaning

solid *adjective*

1 *(of a building, part of a building, etc: The walls of the house are remarkably solid—you can hear hardly any noise through them.)* **strong, substantial, strongly built, well-built, sturdy.**

2 *(of gold, silver, etc: The ring is made of solid gold.)* **pure, unalloyed.**

3 *(of ground, land, etc: The pilot tried to land on some solid ground rather than the sea.)* **firm, hard.**

4 *(of a period of time: We will have to wait a solid day for another train.)* **whole, entire, complete.**

5 *(of work, effort, etc: Some solid work is required to finish these orders in time.)* **substantial, sound, real.**

6 *(of a person: The councillor appealed to the solid citizens of the town to support him.)* **upright, upstanding, decent, worthy, law-abiding.**

7 *(of a business company: Molly joined a solid company that had been in business for decades.)* **sound, secure, reliable dependable, creditworthy.**

8 *(of an argument, reasoning, etc: If you want the committee to accept your proposal you will have to put forward a solid argument.)* **sound, well-founded, cogent, convincing.**

9 *(of a relationship: They have established a solid partnership over the years.)* **stable, firm.**

10 *(of support for a cause, person, etc: Support for the protest group is unlikely to remain solid.)* **united, unanimous, undivided.**

Read the following passage carefully, paying particular attention to the words in bold type.

'These are really **solid** houses in this street,' said Joe, looking at the kitchen of Kay's parents' house and admiring some candlesticks made of **solid** silver. 'Yes, they were built to last,' replied Kay, as she waited for some soup to defrost. This would take some time as it was still a **solid** block but, as Kay had pointed out, they had plenty of time. Their friend, June, was staying with Kay and she usually took a **solid** hour to get dressed and put her makeup on. They had all three just finished college, having put in a great deal of **solid** work while studying for the past three years. Furthermore, they had all three got jobs, which made them feel as though they were about to become **solid** tax-paying citizens. They were all doing different things. Kay was going to be a trainee accountant with a good, **solid** company, which had been recommended by her father. Joe was going to do a course in journalism and June had got a job in theatre design, despite the **solid** arguments put forward by her parents as to why she should seek a career in something more reliable. Since their friendship was **solid**, having lasted through their college years, they were sure that they would keep in touch, in spite of their varied careers. This afternoon they were off to see the local football team play. Somehow, support for it remained **solid** although they had not played well for some time.

Exercise 1

Find a suitable word that is similar in meaning to 'solid' for each blank.

'These are really **1.** ____________ houses in this street, 'said Joe, looking at the kitchen of Kay's parents' house and admiring some candlesticks made of **2.** ____________ silver. 'Yes, they were built to last,' replied Kay, as she waited for some soup to defrost. This would take some time as it was still a **3.** ____________ block but, as Kay had pointed out, they had plenty of time. Their friend, June, was staying with Kay and she usually took a **4.** ____________ hour to get dressed and put her makeup on. They had all three just finished college, having put in a great deal of **5.** ____________ work while studying for the past three years. Furthermore, they had all three got jobs, which made them feel as though they were about to become **6.** ____________ tax-paying citizens. They were all doing different things. Kay was going to be a trainee accountant with a good, **7.** ____________ company, which had been recommended by her father. Joe was going to do a course in journalism and June had got a job in theatre design, despite the **8.** ____________ arguments put forward by her parents as to why she should seek a career in something more reliable. Since their friendship was **9.** ____________, having lasted through their college years, they were sure that they would keep in touch, in spite of their varied careers. This afternoon they were off to see the local football team play. Somehow, support for it remained **10.** ____________ although they had not played well for some time.

Exercise 2

Rewrite the following sentences, replacing the words in bold with a suitable alternative.

1 A lot of **solid** work requires to be done on this garden.

2 We thought it was a safe, **solid** company but it has gone bankrupt.

3 The floors of this old house are really **solid**.

4 We put forward **solid** reasons for extending the village hall.

5 Is that pendant **solid** gold?

6 Jenny and Jim have had a **solid** relationship since their schooldays, but they have now quarrelled.

7 This dessert is still **solid**—we'll have to thaw it.

8 Support for the government remained **solid** throughout the election.

9 We waited two **solid** hours for a bus.

10 Len used to be a rebellious student, but now he's a **solid** member of the community.

3

Kitchen Accidents

Read the following passage carefully, paying particular attention to the words in bold type.

Anna had cut herself on something **sharp** when she was cleaning the kitchen floor. It had been very sore, causing her to give a **sharp** cry. Unfortunately, the wound was in exactly the same place where she had cut herself the day before with a kitchen knife which had caused a **sharp** pain in her palm. At the time her mother had rebuked her for being careless, saying that someone as **sharp** as Mary should be able to avoid such accidents. Although they loved each other dearly, there was a **sharp** difference between the personalities of Anna's mother and father, and her father had sympathized with Anna for having hurt herself. This time Anna had cleaned the wound and applied a plaster, which she hoped her mother would not see. She was now drinking some lemonade that was rather **sharp** and telling her father about her wound, feeling comforted by his concern. However, there was a **sharp** change of subject when Anna's mother entered the room. Unlike either Anna or her father, she was a **sharp** dresser and was looking elegant in her business suit. A lawyer, she had just finished a court case in which her client, a jeweller, had been accused of **sharp** practices. During the case she had been quite **sharp** with her family because she had been very tired. Now that it was over and her client found innocent, she was able to relax and apologized to them for her bad temper.

Know the Meaning

sharp *adjective*

1 *(of something with a pointed or cutting edge: Jean was walking on the sand and injured her foot on something sharp.)* **pointed, spiky.**

2 *(of a cry, etc: The animal gave a sharp cry of pain.)* **shrill, high-pitched, piercing, penetrating.**

3 *(of a pain, etc: As she ran, she got a sharp pain in her side.)* **stabbing, piercing, acute, intense.**

4 *(of a person, with reference to intelligence: The boy is very sharp for his age.)* **clever, intelligent, bright, quick, quick-witted.**

5 *(of a difference: There was a sharp distinction between the two teaching methods.)* **marked, clear, clear-cut, well-defined.**

6 *(of food or drink: The lemon pudding was too sharp for my taste.)* **sour, tart, acid.**

7 *(of a change, etc: There was a sharp change in training methods under the new coach.)* **sudden, abrupt, rapid.**

8 *(of a person, with reference to dress: Tim is a sharp dresser—he always buys the latest fashions.)* **smart, stylish, chic, fashionable.**

9 *(of a person, such as a trader, etc: The market trader was found guilty of sharp practices.)* **dishonest, fraudulent, unscrupulous, underhand.**

10 *(of a person or of a remark, etc: The teacher delivered a sharp rebuke to the children.)* **curt, brusque, short, snappish, caustic.**

Exercise 1

Find a suitable word that is similar in meaning to 'sharp' for each blank.

Anna had cut herself on something **1.** ____________ when she was cleaning the kitchen floor. It had been very sore, causing her to give a **2.** ____________ cry. Unfortunately, the wound was in exactly the same place where she had cut herself the day before with a kitchen knife which had caused a **3.** ____________ pain in her palm. At the time her mother had rebuked her for being careless, saying that someone as **4.** ____________ as Mary should be able to avoid such accidents. Although they loved each other dearly, there was a **5.** ____________ difference between the personalities of Anna's mother and father, and her father had sympathized with Anna for having hurt herself. This time Anna had cleaned the wound and applied a plaster, which she hoped her mother would not see. She was now drinking some lemonade that was rather **6.** ____________ and telling her father about her wound, feeling comforted by his concern. However, there was a **7.** ____________ change of subject when Anna's mother entered the room. Unlike either Anna or her father, she was a **8.** ____________ dresser and was looking elegant in her business suit. A lawyer, she had just finished a court case in which her client, a jeweller, had been accused of **9.** ____________ practices. During the case she had been quite **10.** ____________ with her family because she had been very tired. Now that it was over and her client found innocent, she was able to relax and apologized to them for her bad temper.

Exercise 2

Rewrite the following sentences, replacing the words in bold with a suitable alternative.

1 There is a **sharp** difference of opinion between the two sides.

2 We took a **sharp** change in direction.

3 Larry cut his finger on something **sharp** when tidying up his tool shed.

4 Julie used to wear jeans all the time, but she's a really **sharp** dresser now.

5 Jill gave a **sharp** cry when she stood on a nail.

6 I can't believe that my accountant was accused of **sharp** practices—he's extremely honest.

7 Don took a **sharp** pain in his chest and thought that he was having a heart attack.

8 Jim had a headache and was unusually **sharp** with the children.

9 The little girl is very **sharp** and realized what the adults were talking about.

10 The lime drink was too dilute and not **sharp** enough.

4 A Weekend Trip

Know the Meaning

hold *verb*

1 *(of weather: The fine spell of weather is not expected to hold beyond tomorrow.)* **continue, last, go on, stay, remain.**

2 *(of a person: to hold someone responsible for something.)* **consider, regard as, view as, judge.**

3 *(of a person, piece of writing, speech, etc: The book did not hold the child's interest for long.)* **keep, retain, occupy, engage.**

4 *(of a person: The child held his mother's hand as they crossed the street.)* **grip, clutch, grasp, clasp.**

5 *(of a person or group, with reference to a meeting, assembly, etc: The council decided to hold a public meeting about the new road.)* **call, convene, conduct, have.**

6 *(of a place or object, with reference to memories, associations, etc: That area of the country holds rather sad memories for my mother.)* **have, possess, contain, retain, harbour.**

7 *(of an object, with reference to weight, etc: I don't think that stool will hold Bob's weight—he's so heavy.)* **bear, carry, take, support.**

8 *(of a person, with reference to an opinion, belief, etc: We hold that we should postpone the meeting.)* **think, believe, feel, consider, be of the opinion that.**

9 *(of a person, with reference to a job, position, etc: Does Pat still hold the position of club treasurer?)* **be in, occupy, fill.**

10 *(of a rule, condition, etc: The same conditions hold as last time.)* **stand, apply, be in force, be in effect.**

Read the following passage carefully, paying particular attention to the words in bold type.

'Do you think the good weather **will hold** during the weekend?' asked Mr Taylor. 'It's supposed to stay warm and fine until the end of next week at least,' replied his wife. 'We **can hold** the weather forecast people responsible if it rains.' Mr Taylor went on to say, 'I was wondering about going away for the weekend since the weather's so fine. Where would you like to go?' Usually, the four Taylor children paid little attention to what their parents were saying. However, on this occasion their father had no difficulty in **holding** their attention. His younger daughter, Meg, **held** his hand while his elder son, Jim, suggested that they **held** a family meeting to decide where to go. Mr Taylor said that there was no time for that and that, anyhow, he and their mother would like to go to Hopetown which **held** so many happy family memories. At this, Jim pointed out that he had once hurt his leg at Hopetown when a box on which he had been sitting, had failed to **hold** his weight. His father replied that Jim was accident-prone. 'I **hold** that we take a vote on it,' he said, who liked a good argument and **held** the post of president of his school debating society. They did and Jim lost. On their way to Hopetown, Mr Taylor said, 'Remember the family rule still **holds**.' Meg asked, 'What's that?' 'We all have to enjoy ourselves!' cried the Taylor parents together.

Exercise 1

Find a suitable word that is similar in meaning to 'hold' for each blank.

'Do you think the good weather will **1.** ____________ during the weekend?' asked Mr Taylor. 'It's supposed to stay warm and fine until the end of next week at least,' replied his wife. 'We can **2.** ____________ the weather forecast people responsible if it rains.' Mr Taylor went on to say, 'I was wondering about going away for the weekend since the weather's so fine. Where would you like to go?' Usually, the four Taylor children paid little attention to what their parents were saying. However, on this occasion their father had no difficulty in **3.** ____________ their attention. His younger daughter, Meg, **4.** ____________ his hand while his elder son, Jim, suggested that they **5.** ____________ a family meeting to decide where to go. Mr Taylor said that there was no time for that and that, anyhow, he and their mother would like to go to Hopetown, which **6.** ____________ so many happy family memories. At this, Jim pointed out that he had once hurt his leg at Hopetown when a box on which he had been sitting, had failed to **7.** ____________ his weight. His father replied that Jim was accident-prone. 'I **8** ____________ that we take a vote on it,' he said, who liked a good argument and **9.** ____________ the post of president of his school debating society. They did and Jim lost. On their way to Hopetown, Mr Taylor said, 'Remember the family rule still **10.** ____________.' Meg asked, 'What's that?' 'We all have to enjoy ourselves!' cried the Taylor parents together.

Exercise 2

Rewrite the following sentences, replacing the words in bold with a suitable alternative.

1 I don't think that small folding chair **will hold** Dick's weight.

2 The old house **holds** lots of happy associations for me.

3 We hope that this sunny weather **holds** until our holiday.

4 Jeff still **holds** that George is guilty.

5 It is unfair to **hold** Fred accountable for the accident.

6 Rita **holds** an important post in the civil service.

7 The lecturer was boring and **could** not **hold** the audience's attention.

8 The same regulation still **holds**.

9 Meg **held** her boyfriend's hand as they walked down the street.

10 We **held** a meeting of the residents of the village to discuss traffic problems.

5

A Spanish Trip Is Planned

Read the following passage carefully, paying particular attention to the words in bold type.

Jim had taken a part-time job as a hotel door-keeper because he wanted to have enough money to **cover** a trip to Spain. He must remember to take out insurance to **cover** theft and medical expenses. Since he was learning Spanish at college, he wanted to get to know more about the country. He had taken out several library books, all **covering** different aspects of the country. One of his friends, who was spending a year in south-west France, had a car and it was their intention to drive to southern Spain. They had yet to work out how many kilometres they **could cover** each day. Last time he had been in France it had been near one of the ski resorts and, of course, the ground **had been covered** in snow. However, they were going in mid-summer when it was liable to be very hot in the south. Being fair-skinned, Jim would have to **cover** his skin in a high-factor sunscreen. Today he had been told to **cover** the hotel front entrance and try to keep out journalists and photographers trying to **cover** a story about one of their guests. This was a film star who had been attacked in the street. Usually she went around **covered** in silk and furs but today she was avoiding attention in jeans and a sweater. It was difficult to keep the press out. Jim had just spotted a photographer trying to enter with a pile of clothes **covering** his camera.

Know the Meaning

cover *verb*

1 *(of a person, with reference to payment: We had just enough money to cover lunch.)* **pay for, pay the cost of, be enough for, be sufficient for.**

2 *(of an insurance policy: Does the policy cover delayed flights?)* **insure against, protect against, compensate for.**

3 *(of a statement, article, etc: The report covered all aspects of the business.)* **deal with, take in, include, comprise.**

4 *(of a driver, walker, etc: The drivers estimated how many miles they could cover in an hour.)* **travel, complete, do.**

5 *(of flowers, snow, etc: A mass of bluebells covered the ground.)* **overspread, lie over, carpet, blanket.**

6 *(of a person, with reference to a cream, etc: She covered her face in moisturizing cream.)* **smear, coat, daub.**

7 *(of a policeman, guard, etc: The police were covering all the entrances to the bank.)* **guard, defend, shield, protect.**

8 *(of a journalist, etc: The journalists had been sent to cover the mining disaster.)* **report on, write about.**

9 *(of a garment, etc: The child was covered in a woollen garment.)* **dress, clothe, attire.**

10 *(of a person, with reference to concealment: The prisoner covered his head with his hands as he left the court.)* **shield, hide, conceal.**

Exercise 1

Find a suitable word that is similar in meaning to 'cover' for each blank.

Jim had taken a part-time job as a hotel door-keeper because he wanted to have enough money to **1.** ____________ a trip to Spain. He must remember to take out insurance to **2.** ____________ theft and medical expenses. Since he was learning Spanish at college, he wanted to get to know more about the country. He had taken out several library books, all **3.** ____________ different aspects of the country. One of his friends, who was spending a year in south-west France, had a car and it was their intention to drive to southern Spain. They had yet to work out how many kilometres they could **4.** ____________ each day. Last time he had been in France it had been near one of the ski resorts and, of course, the ground had been **5.** ____________ in snow. However, they were going in mid-summer when it was liable to be very hot in the south. Being fair-skinned, Jim would have to **6.** ____________ his skin in a high-factor sunscreen. Today he had been told to **7.** ____________ the hotel front entrance and try to keep out journalists and photographers trying to **8.** ____________ a story about one of their guests. This was a film star who had been attacked in the street. Usually she went around **9.** ____________ in silk and furs but today she was avoiding attention in jeans and a sweater. It was difficult to keep the press out. Jim had just spotted a photographer trying to enter with a pile of clothes **10.** ____________ his camera.

Exercise 2

Rewrite the following sentences, replacing the words in bold with a suitable alternative.

1 The ground **was covered** in a thick frost.

____

2 The trainee journalist is sent to **cover** local weddings.

____

3 Will that money **cover** the cost of the meal?

____

4 The empress **was covered** in costly silks.

____

5 The holiday insurance **didn't cover** us for loss of earnings.

____

6 The film star **covered** her head with a shawl to avoid the cameras.

____

7 The course **covers** the basics of dressmaking.

____

8 Mary **covered** her arms in a cream to soothe the itch.

____

9 They thought that they **could** easily **cover** 200 kilometres in the first day.

____

10 The police **were covering** the security men with guns as they took the money away.

____

6 A House in the Country

Know the Meaning

have *verb*

1 *(of a person, with reference to possessions: The Nathans have three cars.)* **own, possess, maintain.**
2 *(of an object: The cottage has two bedrooms.)* **contain, comprise.**
3 *(of a person or animal, with reference to experiences: Rosie had had a lot of joy in her life.)* **experience, encounter, meet with.**
4 *(of a person: The criminal seemed to have no remorse.)* **express, show, display, demonstrate, exhibit.**
5 *(of a person: The teacher said that she would not have such behaviour in the classroom.)* **allow, permit, tolerate, put up with, stand.**
6 *(of a person, with reference to feelings, doubts, etc: Sue had no doubts about marrying James.)* **feel, entertain, harbour.**
7 *(of a person, with reference to an occasion or event, etc: They had an amusing evening at the funfair.)* **enjoy, experience.**
8 *(of a person, with reference to food: They had lunch around twelve noon.)* **eat, take.**
9 *(of a female person or animal, with reference to reproduction: Molly had her baby in the local maternity hospital.)* **give birth to, be delivered of.**
10 *(of a person, with reference to receiving something: Jane had a lot of gifts when she got married.)* **receive, get, be given, obtain.**

Read the following passage carefully, paying particular attention to the words in bold type.

The Nathans **had** two houses, one in the town and one in the country. The town house was quite small but the one in the country **had** five bedrooms. In fact, they **had had** a lot of trouble finding it, spending several months contacting estate agents, many of whom **had** not **had** the courtesy to send any details of properties. Anne Nathan, saying that she simply **would** not **have** such behaviour, wrote several letters of complaint. When they first saw this house, they **had** absolutely no doubts about it and bought it right away. Frequently they invited friends down for the weekend and they always **had** a good time. The guests usually **had** dinner on Saturday and lunch on Sunday before returning to town. At the moment her husband, Ram, was doing a lot of the work for these weekends because she was heavily pregnant and felt very tired. When she **had** the baby, she was intending to live in the country full time for at least a few months. She **had** already a lot of baby clothes and equipment from friends down there. It was her hope that she could arrange to work from home, going up to town perhaps only once a week. Ram was hoping that he could do the same because they had a lot of computer equipment in the country house. However, he felt that it might take some considerable time to persuade his employers to let him do that. Meanwhile he would just be able to visit family at weekends and holidays.

Exercise 1

Find a suitable word that is similar in meaning to 'have' for each blank.

The Nathans **1.** ____________________ two houses, one in the town and one in the country. The town house was quite small but the one in the country **2.** ____________________ five bedrooms. In fact, they **3.** ____________________ a lot of trouble finding it, spending several months contacting estate agents, many of whom had not **4.** ____________________ the courtesy to send any details of properties. Anne Nathan, saying that she simply would not **5.** ____________________ such behaviour, wrote several letters of complaint. When they first saw this house, they **6.** ____________________ absolutely no doubts about it and bought it right away. Frequently they invited friends down for the weekend and they always **7.** ____________________ a good time. The guests usually **8.** ____________________ dinner on Saturday and lunch on Sunday before returning to town. At the moment her husband Ram was doing a lot of the work for these weekends because she was heavily pregnant and felt very tired. When she **9.** ____________________ the baby, she was intending to live in the country full time for at least a few months. She **10.** ____________________ already a lot of clothes and equipment from friends down there. It was her hope that she could arrange to work from home, going up to town perhaps only once a week. Ram was hoping that he could do the same because they had a lot of computer equipment in the country house. However, he felt that it might take some considerable time to persuade his employers to let him do that. Meanwhile he would just be able to visit family at weekends and holidays.

Exercise 2

Rewrite the following sentences, replacing the words in bold with a suitable alternative.

1 Bill **had** some misgivings about leaving his job.

2 Shall we **have** lunch in the garden?

3 The family **have** four television sets in all.

4 We **had** the most entertaining evening at the new show.

5 The house **has** only one bathroom.

6 Pat **had** her baby in the ambulance on the way to the hospital.

7 Mike **has had** a great deal of disappointment in the last few years.

8 The children **have** a great many gifts at Christmas.

9 The woman who stole the pram **had** no shame.

10 The teacher said that she simply **would** not **have** such untidy work from her pupils.

7

A Great Occasion

Read the following passage carefully, paying particular attention to the words in bold type.

Molly was feeling both excited and nervous. During her college vacation she had been doing secretarial work for a visiting diplomat. Now she had been asked to attend a party at the embassy and this was sure to be a **great** occasion. Apart from anything else, the embassy was a wonderful house with a **great** expanse of lawns going down to a river. Her friends told her that she must describe the occasion in **great** detail to them after the party. At first she had told them that she was too nervous to go since the **great** people from several countries would be there. However, they had told her not to be a **great** fool but to go to the party and enjoy it. 'The **great** thing,' said her friend Eddie, 'is just to be your natural self.' As she was about to leave for the party, her friends came to wish her luck and tell her that she was looking **great**. When she arrived at the party Molly, who was a **great** film enthusiast, was amazed and delighted when she was introduced to one of her favourite film stars. Being an enthusiastic tennis player, she was even more delighted to meet two people who had been **great** tennis players a decade ago. After the party Molly had to admit that she had had a **great** time. She was extremely glad that her friends had persuaded her to go. As promised, she told them all about it.

Know the Meaning

great *adjective*

1 *(of an event, occasion, etc: The ball at the castle was a great occasion.)* **splendid, grand, magnificent.**

2 *(of land, etc: A great stretch of woodland formed part of the estate.)* **large, big, extensive, huge, vast.**

3 *(Joe's mistake caused great confusion. Great damage was caused by the bomb.)* **much, considerable, substantial.**

4 *(of a person: Many of the great people of the land attended the royal ball.)* **top, leading, important, notable, eminent, distinguished.**

5 *(of a person: Alice must be a great idiot to trust Ned again.)* **complete, absolute, utter, total.**

6 *(of a situation, event, etc: The great thing to do is to remain calm. That was a great moment in the history of the club.)* **important, vital, crucial.**

7 *(of a person, with reference to appearance: The bridal couple looked great.)* **attractive, good-looking, beautiful, handsome, wonderful, sensational.**

8 *(of a person: The boys are great cricket fans.)* **enthusiastic, keen, eager, devoted.**

9 *(of a person: Dave used to be one of the country's great cricketers.)* **expert, talented, able, skilful, ace** *(informal)*.

10 *(of an occasion, outing, etc: The children had a great day by the sea.)* **enjoyable, wonderful, marvellous, splendid, terrific, fantastic** *(informal)*.

Exercise 1

Find a suitable word that is similar in meaning to 'great' for each blank.

Molly was feeling both excited and nervous. During her college vacation she had been doing secretarial work for a visiting diplomat. Now she had been asked to attend a party at the embassy and this was sure to be a **1.** ____________ occasion. Apart from anything else, the embassy was a wonderful house with a **2.** ____________ expanse of lawns going down to a river. Her friends told her that she must describe the occasion in **3.** ____________ detail to them after the party. At first she had told them that she was too nervous to go since the **4.** ____________ people from several countries would be there. However, they had told her not to be a **5.** ____________ fool but to go to the party and enjoy it. 'The **6.** ____________ thing,' said her friend Eddie, 'is just to be your natural self.' As she was about to leave for the party, her friends came to wish her luck and tell her that she was looking **7.** ____________. When she arrived at the party Molly, who was a **8.** ____________ film enthusiast, was amazed and delighted when she was introduced to one of her favourite film stars. Being an enthusiastic tennis player, she was even more delighted to meet two people who had been **9.** ____________ tennis players a decade ago. After the party Molly had to admit that she had had a **10.** ____________ time. She was extremely glad that her friends had persuaded her to go. As promised, she told them all about it.

Exercise 2

Rewrite the following sentences, replacing the words in bold with a suitable alternative.

1 Fred is a **great** idiot to risk cheating in the exam.

2 Adam looked **great** in his evening suit.

3 A **great** banquet was to be held at the palace.

4 Many of the teenagers are **great** followers of the local football team.

5 There was a **great** stretch of water in the valley below.

6 Mary is a **great** sprinter and easily won the race.

7 Tom's actions caused **great** trouble for the family.

8 We saw a really **great** show at the theatre.

9 Many of the **great** people in the land were invited to the state banquet.

10 The **great** thing to remember is that you can easily win the match.

8 Moving House

Know the Meaning

move *verb*

1 *(of a person, with reference to accommodation: I didn't realize that our neighbours were moving.)* **move house, move out, move away, relocate.**

2 *(of a person, with reference to a suggestion, proposal, etc: Sheila moved that we cancel the party.)* **suggest, propose, advocate, recommend.**

3 *(often in passive with reference to a person: The girls were moved to hysterical laughter by the antics of the clown.)* **rouse, stir, prompt, lead.**

4 *(with reference to a person: You won't move George on any issue once he had made his mind up.)* **change, alter, budge.**

5 *(Medical research has moved very rapidly in recent years.)* **progress, advance, proceed, move on.**

6 *(with reference to a person: The tourists were moved by the sight of the beggars.)* **affect, touch, upset.**

7 *(of a person: You will have to move rapidly if you want to buy Colin's car—several people are interested in it.)* **act, take action, do something.**

8 *(of a person, with reference to an object: We moved the table from the kitchen to the dining-room.)* **transport, transfer, shift.**

9 *(of a person: We moved from shop to shop looking for Molly.)* **walk, pass, go, proceed.**

10 *(usually in passive) (of a person: Peter was only moved to look for other accommodation when his landlord gave him notice.)* **motivate, drive, rouse, spur on.**

Read the following passage carefully, paying particular attention to the words in bold type.

The Wang family were about to **move** because their house was no longer big enough for them. When their parents first **moved** it, the idea of leaving **moved** the Wang children to tears. They had tried to persuade their parents not to go, but nothing **could move** their father's attitude. One of the problems was that he was going to work from home some of the time and needed a room to use as a study. Technology **moves** fast nowadays and many people, who were equipped with home computers, were in a similar position. Their mother **was moved** by the children's reaction to leaving the family home, but they had suddenly found a house which they liked and felt that they **should move** immediately before someone else bought it. Now the day had come when they were to leave. The removal men had arrived in a large van and **were** now **moving** their possessions from one house to another. Mrs Wang was so afraid that they might break something valuable that she kept **moving** from room to room to make sure that everything was all right. It seemed as though the men took many breaks and only worked when they felt **moved** to do so. Although the children were still feeling sad and went to say goodbye to their bedrooms and the garden, they were also beginning to look forward to living in their new house, which was just a few streets away. At least they would all have more room.

Exercise 1

Find a suitable word that is similar in meaning to 'move' for each blank.

The Wang family were about to **1.** ____________________ because their house was no longer big enough for them. When their parents first **2.** ____________________ it, the idea of leaving **3.** ____________________ the Wang children to tears. They had tried to persuade their parents not to go, but nothing could **4.** ____________________ their father's attitude. One of the problems was that he was going to work from home some of the time and needed a room to use as a study. Technology **5.** ____________________ fast nowadays and many people, who were equipped with home computers, were in a similar position. Their mother **6.** ____________________ by the children's reaction to leaving the family home, but they had suddenly found a house which they liked and felt that they should **7.** ____________________ immediately before someone else bought it. Now the day had come when they were to leave. The removal men had arrived in a large van and were now **8.** ____________________ their possessions from one house to another. Mrs Wang was so afraid that they might break something valuable that she kept **9.** ____________________ from room to room to make sure that everything was all right. It seemed as though the men took many breaks and only worked when they felt **10.** ____________________ to do so. Although the children were still feeling sad and went to say goodbye to their bedrooms and the garden, they were also beginning to look forward to living in their new house, which was just a few streets away. At least they would all have more room.

Exercise 2

Rewrite the following sentences, replacing the words in bold with a suitable alternative.

1 Computer technology **moves** very quickly.

2 The teacher **was moved** by the sight of the little girl's tears.

3 I was sorry to hear that my neighbour intended to **move**.

4 If we want to book this bargain holiday we **must move** fast.

5 The workers **moved** that they have an extra day's holiday.

6 I **moved** my bookcase from the living room to the study.

7 The audience **was moved** to loud laughter by the comedian.

8 We **were moved** to complain when the neighbours held a noisy party in the garden at midnight.

9 No one **will move** Peggy on the matter of private education.

10 The young couple **moved** from room to room, choosing colour schemes for each one.

9

A Postponed Essay

Read the following passage carefully, paying particular attention to the words in bold type.

Paul **set** his books on his desk and looked at the choice of essay subjects. Although none of them appealed to him, he was really going to have to **set** his mind to this essay if he were going to have it finished in time. Before he **set** pen to paper, he decided that he would like some background music and so he went to switch on his CD player. Then he thought that he had better **set** his watch to the right time because he had to phone his friend, Len, at 7 p.m. to **set** a date for their next football training session. That **set** him thinking about the team's next game and how marvellous it would be if they could maintain the goal-scoring record which they **had set** last year. Still, he hadn't started his essay. After he wrote a few lines, he looked through the window to watch the sun **set**. Somehow he just wasn't in the mood for essay writing. Just as he had completed about half a page his sister, Jill, came in, saying that she had made a dessert for dinner which **had** not **set** properly. This reminded him that he had not done any of the household chores which his mother **had set** him this morning. Usually he hated doing household chores, and tried to avoid them as much as possible. However, at the moment, anything was better than essay writing. Off he went to mop the kitchen floor, whistling happily.

Know the Meaning

set *verb*

1 *(with reference to an object: Jack set the box of tools on the garage floor.)* **lay, place, put down, deposit.**

2 *(of a person: Molly is going to have to set her mind to finding a job.)* **apply, direct, turn, concentrate on, focus on.**

3 *(with reference to a pen, brush, etc: Before he set brush to canvas the artist drew a pencil sketch.)* **apply, put, lay.**

4 *(with reference to a device or machine: Jim had to get up early and so he set his alarm clock.)* **adjust, regulate, set right.**

5 *(with reference to an arrangement, meeting, etc: We must set a time for the next match.)* **arrange, fix, settle, decide on.**

6 *(of a person: Bob's action set me wondering about his motive.)* **start, set off, prompt to, cause to.**

7 *(with reference to a sports record, etc: Jim set the club swimming record last year. The course record was set two years ago.)* **establish, fix, set up.**

8 *(of the sun: It was romantic to sit on the beach and watch the sun set behind the horizon.)* **sink, go down.**

9 *(of food: The ice cream is still very soft—it should have set by now.)* **solidify, harden, thicken, jell.**

10 *(of a person, with reference to a task: The lecturer set the students a holiday essay.)* **assign, allocate, give, give out.**

Exercise 1

Find a suitable word that is similar in meaning to 'set' for each blank.

Paul **1.** ______________ his books on his desk and looked at the choice of essay subjects. Although none of them appealed to him, he was really going to have to **2.** ______________ his mind to this essay if he were going to have it finished in time. Before he **3.** ______________ pen to paper, he decided that he would like some background music and so he went to switch on his CD player. Then he thought that he had better **4.** ______________ his watch to the right time because he had to phone his friend, Len, at 7 p.m. to **5.** ______________ a date for their next football training session. That **6.** ______________ him thinking about the team's next game and how marvellous it would be if they could maintain the goal-scoring record which they had **7.** ______________ last year. Still, he hadn't started his essay. After he wrote a few lines, he looked through the window to watch the sun **8.** ______________. Somehow he just wasn't in the mood for essay writing. Just as he had completed about half a page his sister, Jill, came in, saying that she had made a dessert for dinner which had not **9.** ______________ properly. This reminded him that he had not done any of the household chores which his mother had **10.** ______________ him this morning. Usually he hated doing household chores, and tried to avoid them as much as possible. However, at the moment, anything was better than essay writing. Off he went to mop the kitchen floor, whistling happily.

Exercise 2

Rewrite the following sentences, replacing the words in bold with a suitable alternative.

1 Have Meg and Ralph **set** a date for their wedding yet?

____

2 That was a very high standard to **set** for the competition.

____

3 Beth **set** the books on the floor by her desk.

____

4 We sat on the balcony and watched the sun **set** behind the horizon.

____

5 I'm sure that if you **set** your mind to it, you can win.

____

6 This jelly **has** not **set** yet.

____

7 Phil likes to make several pencil drawings of his subject before he **sets** brush to canvas.

____

8 We **have** all **been set** different tasks as a punishment.

____

9 Before we leave we **should set** our watches so that they all read the same time.

____

10 Alice's reaction **set** Joe to doubting her innocence.

____

10 Wild Country

Know the Meaning

wild *adjective*

1 *(of an idea, plan, etc: When Pam decided to backpack round the world, her parents thought it was a wild notion.)* **mad, crazy, rash, foolhardy, madcap.**

2 *(of a territory, terrain, etc: It was wild terrain up there.)* **desolate, barren, uncivilized, unpopulated, uncultivated.**

3 *(of a person, with reference to behaviour, etc: The children indulged in some rather wild behaviour when their parents were absent.)* **disorderly unrestricted, unrestrained, uncontrolled, undisciplined.**

4 *(of a guess: I didn't know which direction to go in at the crossroads—I took a wild guess.)* **random, haphazard, hit-or-miss, uninformed.**

5 *(of a person: Sally was wild with joy when she got engaged.)* **beside oneself, frantic, frenzied, hysterical.**

6 *(of a person, with reference to a hobby, etc: Pam's little sister is wild about pop music.)* **enthusiastic, mad** *(informal)*, **crazy** *(informal)*.

7 *(of a person, tribe, etc: Until recently the area was occupied by a wild people.)* **savage, fierce, uncivilized, barbaric, primitive.**

8 *(of an animal: The woods were full of wild animals.)* **undomesticated, untamed.**

9 *(of weather: The sailors encountered some wild weather.)* **stormy, rough, blustery, turbulent.**

10 *(of hair: Her hair was wild, having been tossed about by the wind.)* **untidy, dishevelled.**

Read the following passage carefully, paying particular attention to the words in bold type.

The Lawson family had taken a holiday cottage in a very remote part of the country. Many of their friends thought it was a **wild** idea and urged them to get a house nearer a town. 'It's **wild** country out there,' said Mike Lawson's friend Derek. Mike replied, 'We want somewhere really quiet where the children can be as **wild** as they like.' The Lawsons knew little about the area, having taken a **wild** guess about where would meet their requirements. When the parents told their children, Jane, Rick and Craig, about the holiday, they all went **wild** with delight. Jane was even more pleased because she was allowed to take along her friend, Carol, and Carol was **wild** about anything to do with nature. Craig, who was only six years old, wanted to know if there would be **wild** tribes where they were going. 'It's not that remote!' said his mother, Freda. 'The local people will be much like us.' Craig looked disappointed until his father said, 'Never mind! There are sure to be some **wild** animals there.' It was time to set off. When they arrived at their holiday house it was a really **wild** night with heavy rain and strong winds. When they got out of the car, Carol's curly hair quickly became a **wild** mess but she said, 'I don't care! I'm going to forget about worrying what I look like up here!' Mike replied, 'Good idea!' and they all went to admire their home for the summer.

Exercise 1

Find a suitable word that is similar in meaning to 'wild' for each blank.

The Lawson family had taken a holiday cottage in a very remote part of the country. Many of their friends thought it was a **1.** ________________ idea and urged them to get a house nearer a town. 'It's **2.** ________________ country out there,' said Mike Lawson's friend Derek. Mike replied, 'We want somewhere really quiet where the children can be as **3.** ________________ as they like.' The Lawsons knew little about the area, having taken a **4.** ________________ guess about where would meet their requirements. When the parents told their children, Jane, Rick and Craig, about the holiday, they all went **5.** ________________ with delight. Jane was even more pleased because she was allowed to take along her friend, Carol, and Carol was **6.** ________________ about anything to do with nature. Craig, who was only six years old, wanted to know if there would be **7.** ________________ tribes where they were going. 'It's not that remote!' said his mother, Freda. 'The local people will be much like us.' Craig looked disappointed until his father said, 'Never mind! There are sure to be some **8.** ________________ animals there.' It was time to set off. When they arrived at their holiday house it was a really **9.** ________________ night with heavy rain and strong winds. When they got out of the car, Carol's curly hair quickly became a **10.** ________________ mess but she said, 'I don't care! I'm going to forget about worrying what I look like up here!' Mike replied, 'Good idea!' and they all went to admire their home for the summer.

Exercise 2

Rewrite the following sentences, replacing the words in bold with a suitable alternative.

1 The fans were **wild** with joy when their team won the cup.

2 It was a story about two **wild** tribes who wore skins and lived in caves.

3 Anna is not used to city life—she comes from a very **wild** part of the country.

4 The city children had never seen **wild** animals before.

5 Molly has some **wild** idea about giving up college to become a model.

6. The yachtsmen were not expecting such **wild** weather.

7 Jack led rather a **wild** youth.

8 Sara's hair is always a **wild** mess of curls when it's windy.

9 It was a **wild** guess but, in fact, I was right about the number of miles to town.

10 Sue is **wild** about that dress in the shop window.

11 Revisiting the Past

Read the following passage carefully, paying particular attention to the words in bold type.

'Did daddy use to live here in the **old** days?' asked Alice. The family had come to see the village where their father had been brought up. Her father, Peter, laughed, saying, 'Enough of the old! I'm not that **old**. I'm only 40!' When they were walking past Peter's **old** house he began to feel quite nostalgic. His parents had moved away quite a long time ago. Now his father was dead and his mother was in a home for **old** people. Peter, having stopped to speak to some of the inhabitants, was delighted to discover that many of the village's **old** customs and traditions were still in force. Too often these days, anything from the past was dismissed as being **old** and irrelevant. Inevitably there had been some changes. When Peter lived there, there had been a disused **old** mill but it had been pulled down to make way for a block of flats. The man who had run the post office, although not much over middle age, had been regarded as too **old** for the job and was now retired. Peter decided to go and see him but when they reached his house his wife was embarrassed to receive visitors. Being in the midst of cleaning the house, she was wearing her **old** clothes. After they spent an enjoyable hour with their friends, Peter was distressed that the man who had collected **old** cars no longer lived there. 'Nothing stays the same!' said Peter sadly.

Know the Meaning

old *adjective*

1 *(of time: The play was set in the old days.)* **olden, by-gone, early**.

2 *(of a person: Jock has white hair, but he's not that old.)* **advanced in years, advanced in age**.

3 *(of a place: Mick visited his old home town)* **former, previous**.

4 *(of a person: Rob's mother got very frail and old.)* **elderly, advanced in years, advanced in age, aged, up in years, long in the tooth** *(informal/humorous.)*

5 *(of a custom, etc: Many of the old traditions have died out.)* **age-old, long-established, long-standing, time-honoured**.

6 *(of a convention, rule, etc: The young members of the club said they were tired of all the old conventions.)* **old-fashioned, out-of-date, outdated, outmoded, old-hat** *(informal)*.

7 *(of a broken-down building, etc: The old factory had been empty for years and was now dangerous.)* **dilapidated, run-down, broken-down, ramshackle, tumbledown**.

8 *(of a person: He was considered old for the job.)* **too old, past his/her prime, past it** *(informal)*, **over the hill** *(informal)*.

9 *(of a garment: We wore old clothes to clean out the garage.)* **discarded, cast-off, shabby, worn**.

10 *(of a car: It was a race for old cars.)* **vintage, veteran, antique**.

Exercise 1

Find a suitable word that is similar in meaning to 'old' for each blank.

'Did daddy use to live here in the **1.** ____________ days?' asked Alice. The family had come to see the village where their father had been brought up. Her father, Peter, laughed, saying, 'Enough of the old! I'm not that **2.** ____________. I'm only 40!' When they were walking past Peter's **3.** ____________ house he began to feel quite nostalgic. His parents had moved away quite a long time ago. Now his father was dead and his mother was in a home for **4.** ____________ people. Peter, having stopped to speak to some of the inhabitants, was delighted to discover that many of the village's **5.** ____________ customs and traditions were still in force. Too often these days, anything from the past was dismissed as being **6.** ____________ and irrelevant. Inevitably there had been some changes. When Peter lived there, there had been a disused **7.** ____________ mill but it had been pulled down to make way for a block of flats. The man who had run the post office, although not much over middle age, had been regarded as too **8.** ____________ for the job and was now retired. Peter decided to go and see him but when they reached his house his wife was embarrassed to receive visitors. Being in the midst of cleaning the house, she was wearing her **9.** ____________ clothes. After they spent an enjoyable hour with their friends, Peter was distressed that the man who had collected **10.** ____________ cars no longer lived there. 'Nothing stays the same!' said Peter sadly.

Exercise 2

Rewrite the following sentences, replacing the words in bold with a suitable alternative.

1 Many of the **old** children's games are no longer played.

2 There are a lot of **old** shacks by the railway line.

3 The children were read a story about the **old** days.

4 If the company consider you **old** for the job, they declare you redundant.

5 Paula has quite a wrinkled face, but she's not that **old**.

6 Beth got into **old** clothes to redecorate her bedroom.

7 Wendy felt sad when she saw her **old** house again.

8 Paul made a lot of money for that **old** car.

9 Fred's father is **old**, but he's in good health.

10 The young people said that those **old** rules were no longer relevant.

12 Exam Nerves

Know the Meaning

fail *verb*

1 *(of a person: We never fail to be amazed at Jock's good luck.)* **cease, stop** *(+ -ing: We never stop being amazed at Jock's good luck.)*.

2 *(of a person, with reference to an exam, test, etc: Several students failed the history exam.)* **not pass, be unsuccessful in, not make the grade in**.

3 *(of a plan, scheme, etc: Our scheme to raise money failed.)* **not succeed, be unsuccessful, fall through, be in vain, come to nothing**.

4 *(of light: Let's not put the lamps on until the light fails.)* **fade, grow less, die away, peter out**.

5 *(of a person, system, object, etc: When Pam's father died, she felt that the doctors had failed him.)* **let** (someone) **down, disappoint, desert**.

6 *(of health: When the old lady's health failed, she went into hospital.)* **decline, deteriorate, get worse**.

7 *(of a person: George's father is old and failing rapidly.)* **weaken, grow weak, become feeble**.

8 *(of a crop, harvest, etc: The apple crop failed this year.)* **be unproductive, be inadequate, be insufficient**.

9 *(of a business: Many businesses failed during the recession.)* **go bankrupt, collapse, go bust** *(informal)*, **go under**.

10 *(of a machine or engine: The car's engine failed and we had to walk.)* **break down, stop working, conk out** *(informal)*.

Read the following passage carefully, paying particular attention to the words in bold type.

Jack's mother never **failed** to be surprised at his attitude to his college work. Throughout the term he would be quite calm about it, saying confidently that he was working very hard. However, the week before the exams he always panicked and insisted that he was bound to **fail**. His parents and sister would then make many attempts to calm and remind him of his comments about having worked during the term, but these **failed**. Having been given a few days' study leave, he would read in the garden until the light **failed** and then go to his bedroom and study there until well after midnight. His parents made sure that he ate regular meals and took some exercise but still they felt that they **were failing** him in some way. They were also trying to avoid Jack worrying his grandmother, whose health **was failing**. She had been quite strong a year ago when she came to live with them but now she seemed to **be failing** rapidly. Jack's father had other problems as well. He owned both a farm and a farm shop and neither was doing well. The previous season's crop **had failed** because of drought and the shop looked as though it **would fail** if trade did not improve soon. On the morning of his first exam Jack was sure that the engine of the car was going to **fail**, but all was well. He completed the exams in time and, indeed, passed them all.

Exercise 1

Find a suitable word that is similar in meaning to 'fail' for each blank.

Jack's mother never **1.** ______________ to be surprised at his attitude to his college work. Throughout the term he would be quite calm about it, saying confidently that he was working very hard. However, the week before the exams he always panicked and insisted that he was bound to **2.** ______________. His parents and sister would then make many attempts to calm and remind him of his comments about having worked during the term, but these **3.** ______________. Having been given a few days' study leave, he would read in the garden until the light **4.** ______________ and then go to his bedroom and study there until well after midnight. His parents made sure that he ate regular meals and took some exercise but still they felt that they **5.** ______________ him in some way. They were also trying to avoid Jack worrying his grandmother, whose health **6.** ______________. She had been quite strong a year ago when she came to live with them but now she seemed to **7.** ______________ rapidly. Jack's father had other problems as well. He owned both a farm and a farm shop and neither was doing well. The previous season's crop had **8.** ______________ because of drought and the shop looked as though it would **9.** ______________ if trade did not improve soon. On the morning of his first exam Jack was sure that the engine of the car was going to **10.** ______________, but all was well. He completed the exams in time and, indeed, passed them all.

Exercise 2

Rewrite the following sentences, replacing the words in bold with a suitable alternative.

1 Sam's grandmother's health **has been failing** for some time.

2 The elderly man **has failed** noticeably since coming into hospital.

3 Jane says that she never **fails** to wonder at Sue's self-confidence.

4 The rice crop **failed** because of unusual weather conditions.

5 Laura **failed** the exam because she was ill.

6 Many small businesses **fail** not long after starting up.

7 We didn't expect our plan to **fail**.

8 The washing machine's motor **failed** suddenly.

9 We couldn't finish our tennis game because the light **failed**.

10 Diane was counting on Rob's help but we weren't surprised when he **failed** her.

13

Life on the Farm

Read the following passage carefully, paying particular attention to the words in bold type.

Mike and two of his college friends, Paul and Jerry, had agreed to help a local farmer during their winter holidays, while two of his workers were off ill. Since the work was very **hard**, they were always very tired at the end of the day and unwilling to get up in the morning. This particular morning was worse than usual as it was very cold and the ground was **hard** with frost. As the farmer was rather a **hard** man, they were all afraid of being late, and reluctantly got out of bed. He had already had a few **hard** words for them one morning when they were very slightly late and they did not want to repeat this experience. One thing they all agreed on. Although the problem of what to do when they left college was a **hard** one, the life of a farmer was not for them. Living conditions seemed to be very **hard** and the **hard** facts were that, despite all the work, the farmer did not make much money. The work could be dangerous, too. Paul had received a **hard** kick from a horse, which had left him limping. The farmer, who was pleased that the boys were all **hard** workers, tried to give Paul some brandy for the pain but Paul refused the offer since he never took **hard** liquor. For the most part the friends were glad when they returned to college. That was a much more comfortable life.

Know the Meaning

hard *adjective*

1 *(of work or labour: They found factory work very hard.)* **arduous, strenuous, laborious, tough, difficult.**

2 *(of ground: It had been frosty for several days and the ground was very hard.)* **firm, solid, close-packed, rock-like.**

3 *(of a person: Jock liked to pretend to be a hard man, but he was actually very kind.)* **harsh, hard-hearted, severe, stern, unfeeling.**

4 *(of words: After an exchange of hard words the couple parted.)* **harsh, unkind, angry, acrimonious, hostile.**

5 *(of a problem, etc: The problem of which career to follow was a hard one.)* **difficult, complicated, complex.**

6 *(of a way of life: Life was hard for the peasants.)* **difficult, harsh, tough, uncomfortable, bleak, grim.**

7 *(of facts: The hard facts are that Matt's bankrupt.)* **plain, bare, blunt, unvarnished.**

8 *(of a blow, shock, etc: Tom received a hard blow to his head.)* **severe, violent, forceful, powerful.**

9 *(of a worker: The boss said that his staff were all hard workers.)* **hard-working, diligent, industrious, conscientious.**

10 *(of drink: None of the young men drank hard liquor.)* **alcoholic, strong.**

Exercise 1

Find a suitable word that is similar in meaning to 'hard' for each blank.

Mike and two of his college friends, Paul and Jerry, had agreed to help a local farmer during their winter holidays, while two of his workers were off ill. Since the work was very **1.** ____________________, they were always very tired at the end of the day and unwilling to get up in the morning. This particular morning was worse than usual as it was very cold and the ground was **2.** ____________________ with frost. As the farmer was rather a **3.** ____________________ man, they were all afraid of being late, and reluctantly got out of bed. He had already had a few **4.** ____________________ words for them one morning when they were very slightly late and they did not want to repeat this experience. One thing they all agreed on. Although the problem of what to do when they left college was a **5.** ____________________ one, the life of a farmer was not for them. Living conditions seemed to be very **6.** ____________________ and the **7.** ____________________ facts were that, despite all the work, the farmer did not make much money. The work could be dangerous, too. Paul had received a **8.** ____________________ kick from a horse, which had left him limping. The farmer, who was pleased that the boys were all **9.** ____________________ workers, tried to give Paul some brandy for the pain but Paul refused the offer since he never took **10.** ____________________ liquor. For the most part the friends were glad when they returned to college. That was a much more comfortable life.

Exercise 2

Rewrite the following sentences, replacing the words in bold with a suitable alternative.

1 Knowing which job to take was a **hard** decision.

2 The **hard** facts are that we are going to have to sack some of the staff.

3 Working in the quarry was very **hard** work.

4 In the accident Pat received a **hard** knock on the head.

5 The ground is too **hard** to dig.

6 You will have to prove that you are a **hard** worker to get that job.

7 The new teacher won't accept work handed in late—he seems a very **hard** man.

8 Peter occasionally drinks a glass of wine but he never takes **hard** liquor.

9 His parents had some **hard** words for Oliver when he had a party and wrecked the house.

10 The region had been affected by famine and life was very **hard**.

14 Looking After Uncle Bob

Know the Meaning

heavy *adjective*

1 *(of a responsibility, etc: Looking after their invalid mother is too heavy a responsibility for young teenagers.)* **weighty, onerous, burdensome.**

2 *(of a task, work, etc: They were given heavy tasks.)* **hard, difficult, arduous, demanding.**

3 *(of a load, etc: The work involved carrying heavy loads.)* **weighty, hefty, substantial, bulky.**

4 *(of soil: There is very heavy soil in that region.)* **muddy, sticky, clayey.**

5 *(of a person: Jim is a very heavy man and needs to lose weight.)* **big, large, bulky, stout, fat.**

6 *(of a subject, etc: Len always bought newspapers which dealt with heavy issues.)* **serious, heavyweight, weighty, deep, profound.**

7 *(of traffic, trading, etc: The traffic on the motorway is always heavy.)* **substantial, considerable, abundant.**

8 *(of the sky: The sky was heavy just before the snow started.)* **cloudy, overcast, dark, grey.**

9 *(of rain: The heavy rain caused flooding in some areas.)* **torrential, pouring** *(used before noun: pouring rain)*, **severe.**

10 *(of the sea: The sea was too heavy to take the boat out.)* **rough, stormy, wild, turbulent.**

Read the following passage carefully, paying particular attention to the words in bold type.

Twins Eric and Carol had been given a very **heavy** responsibility. They had been asked by their parents to go and look after their Uncle Bob for two weeks while they were on holiday from college. The owner of a market garden, he had hurt his back and had to rest. The twins were not pleased. They both found the workload very **heavy** for the tasks included carrying **heavy** boxes of vegetables around and digging. This latter job was particularly difficult as the soil in the area was very **heavy**. They also had to help their uncle in and out of his chair and bed and he was a very **heavy** man. Since their aunt had died just a few months ago, their uncle was still sad and rather silent. When he spoke, he seemed to want to speak about **heavy** subjects, like the economic state of the country. They were sorry for him, but Eric and Carol wanted some fun. However, the nearest town was some miles away and the traffic into it was usually **heavy**. The weather did not help either. Usually they woke to **heavy** skies and frequently there was **heavy** rain before the end of the morning. They heard that fishermen were having difficulty with **heavy** seas. How relieved the twins were when the two weeks came to an end! They were glad to return home and let their cousins do their share of looking after Uncle Bob.

Exercise 1

Find a suitable word that is similar in meaning to 'heavy' for each blank.

Twins Eric and Carol had been given a very **1.** ______________ responsibility. They had been asked by their parents to go and look after their Uncle Bob for two weeks while they were on holiday from college. The owner of a market garden, he had hurt his back and had to rest. The twins were not pleased. They both found the workload very **2.** ______________ for the tasks included carrying **3.** ______________ boxes of vegetables around and digging. This latter job was particularly difficult as the soil in the area was very **4.** ______________. They also had to help their uncle in and out of his chair and bed and he was a very **5.** ______________ man. Since their aunt had died just a few months ago, their uncle was still sad and rather silent. When he spoke, he seemed to want to speak about **6.** ______________ subjects, like the economic state of the country. They were sorry for him, but Eric and Carol wanted some fun. However, the nearest town was some miles away and the traffic into it was usually **7.** ______________. The weather did not help either. Usually they woke to **8.** ______________ skies and frequently there was **9.** ______________ rain before the end of the morning. They heard that fishermen were having difficulty with **10.** ______________ seas. How relieved the twins were when the two weeks came to an end! They were glad to return home and let their cousins do their share of looking after Uncle Bob.

Exercise 2

Rewrite the following sentences, replacing the words in bold with a suitable alternative.

1 Bill was a **heavy** man and the deck chair collapsed under him.

2 The rush hour had not yet started but the traffic out of town was already **heavy**.

3 Taking care of a baby is a **heavy** responsibility for someone so young.

4 The skies are very **heavy**—it's going to rain shortly.

5 We have all been allocated **heavy** jobs.

6 The rain became **heavy** and we ran for shelter.

7 We carried several **heavy** loads of garden rubbish to the refuse truck.

8 The ship ran aground in **heavy** seas.

9 Digging the garden is difficult—the ground is very **heavy**.

10 The play was a bit **heavy** for Bob's taste—he prefers something amusing.

15

A Trip to the Supermarket

Read the following passage carefully, paying particular attention to the words in bold type.

Mrs Chen and her children, Jill and Peter, were going round the supermarket on a Sunday afternoon. The shop was **full** and the children were bored. They had already been there for a **full** hour. How much more could their mother buy? Her trolley was already **full**. She had taken with her a **full** list of all the things which they needed, ticking them off as she put the goods in the trolley. All they could now see was a long line of ticks. Still their mother was looking at various goods. Now she had stopped to speak to someone. It was Mrs Lee, whom they did not really like. She had a very **full** figure which looked even fuller because she always wore very **full** skirts. Mrs Lee liked a good gossip and had a very **full** voice that could be heard from quite a long way away. Mrs Chen suggested that Jill and Peter go to the coffee shop, saying that she would come and get them when she had gone through the check-out. Jill and Peter were not very keen since they had just had breakfast and were **full**. However, they went to the coffee shop only to discover that all the tables were **full**. Worse, Jill knocked over a coffee cup on a table with her bag. The cup was **full** and its contents went all over the skirt of the woman at the table. She was furious. Jill and Peter hurried back to their mother.

Know the Meaning

full *adjective*

1 *(of a room, place, etc: It was Saturday and the shops were full.)* **crowded, packed, chock-a-block.**

2 *(We waited a full week for the parcel to arrive.)* **whole, entire, complete.**

3 *(Mary had bought groceries and her basket was full)* **filled, filled up, filled to capacity, full up, loaded.**

4 *(We need a full list of entrants to the competition.)* **complete, comprehensive, detailed, exhaustive.**

5 *(of the human body: Sara has too full a figure to wear such short skirts.)* **well-built, well-rounded, ample, plump.**

6 *(The dress had a tight bodice and a full skirt.)* **wide.**

7 *(of voice: They were looking for a new choir member with a very full voice.)* **rich, deep, strong.**

8 *(It was not long after lunch and they were still full.)* **replete, sated.**

9 *(The seats in the hall were all full.)* **occupied, taken, in use.**

10 *(These tea cups are full.)* **filled, filled to the brim, brimful.**

Exercise 1

Find a suitable word that is similar in meaning to 'full' for each blank.

Mrs Chen and her children, Jill and Peter, were going round the supermarket on a Sunday afternoon. The shop was **1.** ____________ and the children were bored. They had already been there for a **2.** ____________ hour. How much more could their mother buy? Her trolley was already **3.** ____________. She had taken with her a **4.** ____________ list of all the things which they needed, ticking them off as she put the goods in the trolley. All they could now see was a long line of ticks. Still their mother was looking at various goods. Now she had stopped to speak to someone. It was Mrs Lee, whom they did not really like. She had a very **5.** ____________ figure which looked even fuller because she always wore very **6.** ____________ skirts. Mrs Lee liked a good gossip and had a very **7.** ____________ voice that could be heard from quite a long way away. Mrs Chen suggested that Jill and Peter go to the coffee shop, saying that she would come and get them when she had gone through the check-out. Jill and Peter were not very keen since they had just had breakfast and were **8.** ____________. However, they went to the coffee shop only to discover that all the tables were **9.** ____________. Worse, Jill knocked over a coffee cup on a table with her bag. The cup was **10.** ____________ and its contents went all over the skirt of the woman at the table. She was furious. Jill and Peter hurried back to their mother.

Exercise 2

Rewrite the following sentences, replacing the words in bold with a suitable alternative.

1 The girls were wearing **full** summer skirts.

____

2 Sue had the **full** voice of an opera singer.

____

3 The market was so **full** that we could not see the shops properly.

____

4 We had had a late breakfast and were still feeling very **full**.

____

5 We waited a **full** week for an appointment with the lawyer.

____

6 The seats in the theatre were all **full**.

____

7 The basket was **full** and very heavy.

____

8 The coffee cup was **full** when the child knocked it over.

____

9 Sally is very slender, but her sister had quite a **full** figure.

____

10 You will be sent a **full** list of the books which are required for next year.

____

16 First Time Away from Home

Know the Meaning

light *adjective*

1 *(of clothes or material: The children were wearing light summer clothes.)* **light-weight, thin.**
2 *(of wind: It was hot, but a light breeze kept us cool.)* **slight, mild, gentle, soft.**
3 *(of colour: The walls were light in colour.)* **light-coloured, pale, pastel, muted.**
4 *(of a mark, stain, etc: She indicated the names of the successful applicants with a light pencil mark.)* **faint, slight, indistinct, faded, unclear.**
5 *(of a tap, knock, etc: There was a light knock on the window.)* **gentle, faint, slight, soft.**
6 *(of literature, etc: I've brought some light reading matter.)* **light-hearted, amusing, entertaining.**
7 *(of a spell of illness: The child had a light bout of chickenpox.)* **slight, mild, minor, moderate.**
8 *(of meals: The old lady has very little appetite and can only eat very light meals.)* **small, little, insubstantial, scanty, meagre.**
9 *(of a person, with reference to weight or size: The child has been very ill and is now too light to be healthy.)* **underweight, slight, thin, slim, skinny.**
10 *(of a task: The old lady is still able to do some light household tasks.)* **easy, simple.**

Read the following passage carefully, paying particular attention to the words in bold type.

Judy was excited. This morning she was leaving on a trip to visit her aunt in the south of the country. Since it was usually very warm there in the summer, she had packed all her **light** clothes. Because her aunt lived by the sea, there were often **light** breezes, even on the hottest days, especially in the evenings. Therefore Judy had also packed two heavier sweaters although these had quite a summery look, being **light** in colour. There was an ink mark on one of them, but it was very **light** and she could get it out later. Judy was dancing round her bedroom with excitement when her mother gave a **light** tap on the door. Judy had bought some books of rather a **light** nature to read on the train and she now put them in her bag. A few weeks ago she had had a **light** attack of flu and could still eat only **light** meals. She had lost weight and her mother was worried that she was now much too **light**. As she was still looking rather pale, it would do her good to get some sea air. Her aunt would be glad of her company as she ran a small boarding house, and Judy had said that she would be happy to do some **light** chores. This being her first time away from home, Judy might be a little homesick at first but she would soon recover and have an enjoyable time.

Exercise 1

Find a suitable word that is similar in meaning to 'light' for each blank.

Judy was excited. This morning she was leaving on a trip to visit her aunt in the south of the country. Since it was usually very warm there in the summer, she had packed all her **1.** ____________________ clothes. Because her aunt lived by the sea, there were often **2.** ____________________ breezes, even on the hottest days, especially in the evenings. Therefore Judy had also packed two heavier sweaters although these had quite a summery look, being **3.** ____________________ in colour. There was an ink mark on one of them, but it was very **4.** ____________________ and she could get it out later. Judy was dancing round her bedroom with excitement when her mother gave a **5.** ____________________ tap on the door. Judy had bought some books of rather a **6.** ____________________ nature to read on the train and she now put them in her bag. A few weeks ago she had had a **7.** ____________________ attack of flu and could still eat only **8.** ____________________ meals. She had lost weight and her mother was worried that she was now much too **9.** ____________________. As she was still looking rather pale, it would do her good to get some sea air. Her aunt would be glad of her company as she ran a small boarding house, and Judy had said that she would be happy to do some **10.** ____________________ chores. This being her first time away from home, Judy might be a little homesick at first but she would soon recover and have an enjoyable time.

Exercise 2

Rewrite the following sentences, replacing the words in bold with a suitable alternative.

1 Sara felt a **light** tap on her shoulder.

2 Jim had a **light** attack of food poisoning.

3 We were wearing **light** clothes but the weather turned cold.

4 The child hardly eats anything and has to be coaxed into eating even a **light** meal.

5 A **light** breeze kept the day from being too hot.

6 As a child Jane was very chubby but she's very **light** now.

7 The girls' dresses were **light** in colour.

8 They're employed to do **light** chores such as dusting.

9 This biography is not exactly **light** reading material.

10 I got most of the mud off the football shirt but a **light** stain remained.

17

A Hiking Trip

Read the following passage carefully, paying particular attention to the words in bold type.

'What we need is a few **strong** men!' said Sheila. She and some friends were on a hiking trip and their backpacks seemed to be getting very heavy as the day went on. Her remarks got a **strong** reply from Anna, who came from a family of **strong** women who were all in favour of feminism. 'Nonsense!' she said. 'We can manage very well by ourselves, we don't need men!' Sheila replied that she was just joking to tease Anna. She then turned her attention to the fact that Joan's backpack had a small hole in it. 'They said in the shop that it was made of very **strong** material,' complained Joan, 'and this is the first time I've used it.' Molly, who had a **strong** interest in consumer affairs, told Joan that she must be sure to demand her money back from the shop. 'You certainly have a very **strong** argument for doing so,' agreed Sheila. 'Faulty goods demand **strong** measures.' Being midday, the sunlight was very **strong** and they decided to seek some shade and have a rest and a snack. Most of them had cold drinks but Pat preferred to have some of the **strong** coffee which she had in her Thermos flask. She also had some chocolate with her. This she offered to the others but Molly was on a diet and was **strong** enough to refuse. After the short rest, they continued on their hike, feeling refreshed.

Know the Meaning

strong *adjective*

1 *(of a person, with reference to physical strength): It will take someone strong to lift that heavy weight.)* **powerfully built, muscular, brawny, sturdy.**

2 *(of a reaction, feeling, etc: The speaker's remarks got a strong reaction.)* **forceful, vehement, passionate, intense, fervent.**

3 *(of a person, with reference to personality: Bella had had to be strong to get a job in the all-male team.)* **assertive, forceful, formidable, aggressive, high-powered.**

4 *(of a material: The workers were wearing garments of a strong material.)* **durable, heavy-duty, hard-wearing.**

5 *(of interest, etc: strong interest.)* **keen, enthusiastic, fervent.**

6 *(of a reason, case, etc: strong reasons.)* **forceful, powerful, cogent, convincing, compelling.**

7 *(of action, etc: The police had to take strong action against the vandals.)* **firm, forceful, tough, drastic, severe.**

8 *(of light: strong sunlight.)* **bright, intense, glaring, dazzling.**

9 *(of a drink: This lime squash is too strong.)* **concentrated, undiluted.**

10 *(of a person, with reference to persuasion, temptation, etc: Beth was strong enough to refuse temptation.)* **strong-minded, firm, resolute, determined.**

Exercise 1

Find a suitable word that is similar in meaning to 'strong' for each blank.

'What we need is a few **1.** ________________ men!' said Sheila. She and some friends were on a hiking trip and their backpacks seemed to be getting very heavy as the day went on. Her remarks got a **2.** ________________ reply from Anna, who came from a family of **3.** ________________ women who were all in favour of feminism. 'Nonsense!' she said. 'We can manage very well by ourselves, we don't need men!' Sheila replied that she was just joking to tease Anna. She then turned her attention to the fact that Joan's backpack had a small hole in it. 'They said in the shop that it was made of very **4.** ________________ material,' complained Joan, 'and this is the first time I've used it.' Molly, who had a **5.** ________________ interest in consumer affairs, told Joan that she must be sure to demand her money back from the shop. 'You certainly have a very **6.** ________________ argument for doing so,' agreed Sheila. 'Faulty goods demand **7.** ________________ measures.' Being midday, the sunlight was very **8.** ________________ and they decided to seek some shade and have a rest and a snack. Most of them had cold drinks but Pat preferred to have some of the **9.** ________________ coffee which she had in her Thermos flask. She also had some chocolate with her. This she offered to the others, but Molly was on a diet and was **10.** ________________ enough to refuse. After the short rest, they continued on their hike, feeling refreshed.

Exercise 2

Rewrite the following sentences, replacing the words in bold with a suitable alternative.

1 All the villagers have a **strong** interest in their community.

2 The bad behaviour of some of the students calls for **strong** measures.

3 Two **strong** young men arrived to move the furniture.

4 Working in such a **strong** light hurts my eyes.

5 The speech got a **strong** response from the audience.

6 The child won't take the orange drink if it's **strong**.

7 Freda's **strong** personality makes some people dislike her.

8 Simon was studying and he tried to be **strong** when his friends tried to persuade him to go to a party.

9 We put forward a **strong** argument for not having the building pulled down.

10 You should wear gloves of a **strong** material when disposing of the rubbish.

18 Delayed by Illness

Know the Meaning

keep *verb*

1 *(with reference to a promise, pledge, etc: Don't rely on Phil—he never keeps his promises.)* **abide by, stick to, carry out, fulfil, honour.**

2 *(with reference to a person: Mike just went to the hospital for a check-up, but they kept him for observation.)* **keep** (someone) **in, detain, hold on to.**

3 *(Jean kept working long past retirement age.)* **go on, carry on, continue to.**

4 *(with reference to dependants: Don has to keep a large family on a small salary.)* **provide for, support, maintain.**

5 *(with reference to a custom, etc: The young people don't keep the old traditions.)* **observe, keep to, abide by, follow.**

6 *(of a shopkeeper, etc: The local newsagent keeps a whole range of magazines.)* **sell, stock, have for sale.**

7 *(Jill keeps her lecture notes in the bottom drawer of her desk.)* **store, have.**

8 *(of milk, food, etc: Milk does not keep long in this hot weather.)* **last, stay fresh, keep fresh.**

9 *(with reference to a state or quality: We tried to keep warm by covering ourselves with a blanket. The child cannot keep quiet.)* **stay, remain.**

10 *(with reference to information: Mary's mother was very ill and they tried to keep news of the accident from her.)* **conceal, hide, keep secret, withhold.**

Read the following passage carefully, paying particular attention to the words in bold type.

'What kept you?' Sue asked Bert, rather annoyed. 'You promised to be here by midday and you usually **keep** your promises.' Bert replied, 'Sorry, I couldn't help it. I had to take my father to the hospital with chest pains and they **kept** him in for observation. It seems that he hasn't been feeling well for some time, but he just **kept** working without saying anything. He was worried about going sick and not being able to **keep** my mother and the younger children.' 'That's terrible!' said Sue. 'Can I go and see him?' 'The doctor said that he's not to have many visitors yet. He said only close family were to go and for a short time at that. We better **keep** the hospital rules. You can probably go tomorrow. Meanwhile, I have to take a few things to him. Does your local shop **keep** fruit? He wants some oranges.' 'Yes,' said Sue, 'but I have some that you can take. I **keep** them in a bowl in the kitchen and there's some more fruit in the fridge. It **keeps** longer in there.' Bert thanked her and went to get the fruit. Although he was worried, he was trying to **keep** calm. One thing was quite certain. It was absolutely essential to **keep** his anxiety from his mother as she was worried enough. He left Sue's flat to go over and see her, telling Sue that he would be back after he had delivered his father's things to the hospital.

Exercise 1

Find a suitable word that is similar in meaning to 'keep' for each blank.

'What kept you?' Sue asked Bert, rather annoyed. 'You promised to be here by midday and you usually **1.** ________________ your promises.' Bert replied, 'Sorry, I couldn't help it. I had to take my father to the hospital with chest pains and they **2.** ________________ him in for observation. It seems that he hasn't been feeling well for some time, but he just **3.** ________________ working without saying anything. He was worried about going sick and not being able to **4.** ________________ my mother and the younger children.' 'That's terrible!' said Sue. 'Can I go and see him?' 'The doctor said that he's not to have many visitors yet. He said only close family were to go and for a short time at that. We better **5.** ________________ the hospital rules. You can probably go tomorrow. Meanwhile, I have to take a few things to him. Does your local shop **6.** ________________ fruit? He wants some oranges.' 'Yes,' said Sue, 'but I have some that you can take. I **7.** ________________ them in a bowl in the kitchen and there's some more fruit in the fridge. It **8.** ________________ longer in there.' Bert thanked her and went to get the fruit. Although he was worried, he was trying to **9.** ________________ calm. One thing was quite certain. It was absolutely essential to **10.** ________________ his anxiety from his mother as she was worried enough. He left Sue's flat to go over and see her, telling Sue that he would be back after he had delivered his father's things to the hospital.

Exercise 2

Rewrite the following sentences, replacing the words in bold with a suitable alternative.

1 Susie was punished for failing to **keep** the school rules.

2 We **keep** a supply of logs for the fire in the garden shed.

3 Adam **kept** his promise to his late father and studied medicine.

4 The butter will **keep** longer in the fridge.

5 When Bill went to hospital he didn't think that the doctor would **keep** him there.

6 We sheltered in a barn to **keep** dry in the storm.

7 Their mother **keeps** worrying about Alan and Polly, even though they're grown-up and doing well.

8 Joe is worried about his daughter being so late but he's trying to **keep** his concern from his wife.

9 The local shop **keeps** milk and bread.

10 Rose and John are having a baby but I don't know how John will afford to **keep** a family.

19

Observant Henry

Read the following passage carefully, paying particular attention to the words in bold type.

Will and his **close** friend, Henry, were just coming out of their local football ground. It had been a **close** game and had fittingly ended in a draw. Now they were on their way to Henry's flat which was **close** to the football ground. It was a very **close** day and they were going in search of a cool drink. As Henry was putting his key in the door, he looked curiously at the man coming out of the flat next door. When the man had gone, Henry said, 'That man bears a **close** resemblance to the one featured on a TV crime programme last night. He's wanted for armed robbery.' 'I saw the programme' said Will, 'but I wasn't paying very **close** attention to it and I didn't get a good look at the man.' Henry thought of phoning the police but decided to ask one of his neighbours quite casually if she knew their new neighbour. 'No,' she said. 'I tried to chat to him but he was very **close** about where he had come from and what he was doing. He is also **close** with money—he wouldn't give a donation to charity.' Then Henry felt it was his duty to phone the police, giving them a **close** description of the man. A few hours later he heard a lot of noise and saw a police van at the door. Then the police rang to tell him that the man was now under **close** arrest.

Know the Meaning

close *adjective*

1 *(of friends: Jane and Lucy had been close friends all their lives.)* **bosom, good, intimate, devoted, pally** *(informal)*.

2 *(of a competition, etc: The last set of the tennis tournament was close.)* **evenly-matched, tight, hard-fought, neck-and-neck.**

3 *(of a building, place, etc: We could visit Jan—her house is quite close.)* **near, nearby.**

4 *(of weather: The weather was very close and gave Mary a headache.)* **muggy, stuffy, airless, oppressive.**

5 *(of a likeness: That woman bears a close resemblance to someone I know.)* **marked, strong, distinct, pronounced.**

6 *(of attention, etc: We didn't pay very close attention to the directions and got lost.)* **careful, assiduous.**

7 *(of a person, with reference to information: Anna is very close about her past.)* **secretive, unforthcoming, guarded uncommunicative, close-lipped.**

8 *(of a person with reference to money: Old Joe is very wealthy, but he is very close with his wealth.)* **mean, miserly, stingy, tight, tight-fisted.**

9 *(of a description, report, etc: The driver was not able to give a close description of the accident.)* **accurate, precise, exact, true.**

10 *(The accused was kept under close arrest until he could be charged.)* **tight, secure, strict.**

Exercise 1

Find a suitable word that is similar in meaning to 'close' for each blank.

Will and his **1.** ____________________ friend, Henry, were just coming out of their local football ground. It had been a **2.** ____________________ game and had fittingly ended in a draw. Now they were on their way to Henry's flat which was **3.** ____________________ to the football ground. It was a very **4.** ____________________ day and they were going in search of a cool drink. As Henry was putting his key in the door, he looked curiously at the man coming out of the flat next door. When the man had gone, Henry said, 'That man bears a **5.** ____________________ resemblance to the one featured on a TV crime programme last night. He's wanted for armed robbery.' 'I saw the programme,' said Will, 'but I wasn't paying very **6.** ____________________ attention to it and I didn't get a good look at the man.' Henry thought of phoning the police but decided to ask one of his neighbours quite casually if she knew their new neighbour. 'No,' she said. 'I tried to chat to him but he was very **7.** ____________________ about where he had come from and what he was doing. He is also **8.** ____________________ with money—he wouldn't give a donation to charity.' Then Henry felt it was his duty to phone the police, giving them a **9.** ____________________ description of the man. A few hours later he heard a lot of noise and saw a police van at the door. Then the police rang to tell him that the man was now under **10.** ____________________ arrest.

Exercise 2

Rewrite the following sentences, replacing the words in bold with a suitable alternative.

1 Martin is very **close** about the details of his childhood.

____

2 Peggy is too **close** with her money to contribute to Stan's birthday present.

____

3 The two girls had been **close** friends since childhood.

____

4 I was quite far away from the car crash and so I was unable to give a **close** description of it.

____

5 The match was **close** but our team won in the closing minutes.

____

6 He is on a charge of murder and so will be kept under **close** confinement.

____

7 We could go to the supermarket now—it's quite **close**.

____

8 We were told to pay **close** attention to what the teacher was saying.

____

9 **Close** days like this always make Lucy feel tired.

____

10 That vase bears a **close** resemblance to the one that was stolen from my house.

____

20 An Island Visit

Know the Meaning

rough *adjective*

1 *(of a period of time, situation, etc: Will's had a rough few months since he lost his job.)* **hard, difficult, tough, unpleasant.**

2 *(of a person: Bill's parents were worried because he seemed to have some rough friends.)* **uncouth, coarse, uncivilized.**

3 *(of a voice: Your voice sounds rather rough – do you have a cold?)* **harsh, husky, hoarse.**

4 *(of a guess, estimation, etc: At a rough calculation the town is about 40 kilometres away.)* **approximate, vague, loose, imprecise, inexact.**

5 *(of the sea: The ocean was quite rough when the boat set out.)* **choppy, turbulent, heavy.**

6 *(of weather: The weather was very rough when we began our cruise.)* **stormy, wild, violent.**

7 *(of material, an animal's coat, etc: The dog had a rough, brown coat. The cloth had a very rough finish.)* **shaggy, hairy, bushy, fuzzy.**

8 *(informal) (of a person: Sue had had flu and is still feeling rather rough.)* **ill, unwell, sick, off colour.**

9 *(of words, etc: The farmer had few rough words for the boys who stole his apples.)* **harsh, stern, sharp, angry.**

10 *(of a drawing, plan, etc: The artist made a few rough sketches before painting Beth's portrait.)* **rudimentary, basic, crude, unfinished.**

Read the following passage carefully, paying particular attention to the words in bold type.

Leo and Mick were on holiday and wished to visit a small island which had a ruined castle and a bird sanctuary. They were advised to ask Hector, one of the fishermen, if he would take them.'He's had a **rough** time recently and could do with the money. You might think he's rather a **rough** character, but he's very pleasant,' they were told. When they met Hector, they found that he had such a **rough** voice that they could hardly understand him. At a **rough** estimate they thought that he might be about 35 but he could be any age. Hector said that he would take them there in his small boat next day but warned that the sea could be quite **rough**. In fact next day the weather was so **rough** indeed that Leo thought that Hector wouldn't want to go. However, he was waiting for them by the shore, a dog with a **rough** black coat, having come to see them off. It wasn't a good journey. Mick started to feel very **rough** with the rocking of the boat. He was so glad to see land that he jumped up suddenly and nearly overturned the boat. Hector had a few **rough** words to say to him. Fortunately, the weather cleared while they were on the island and they were able to make a few **rough** sketches of the castle and the birds. It seemed a very short time before Hector returned for them.

Exercise 1

Find a suitable word that is similar in meaning to 'rough' for each blank.

Leo and Mick were on holiday and wished to visit a small island which had a ruined castle and a bird sanctuary. They were advised to ask Hector, one of the fishermen, if he would take them. 'He's had a **1.** ________________ time recently and could do with the money. You might think he's rather a **2.** ________________ character, but he's very pleasant,' they were told. When they met Hector, they found that he had such a **3.** ________________ voice that they could hardly understand him. At a **4.** ________________ estimate they thought that he might be about 35 but he could be any age. Hector said that he would take them there in his small boat next day but warned that the sea could be quite **5.** ________________. In fact next day the weather was so **6.** ________________ indeed that Leo thought that Hector wouldn't want to go. However, he was waiting for them by the shore, a dog with a **7.** ________________ black coat, having come to see them off. It wasn't a good journey. Mick started to feel very **8.** ________________ with the rocking of the boat. He was so glad to see land that he jumped up suddenly and nearly overturned the boat. Hector had a few **9.** ________________ words to say to him. Fortunately, the weather cleared while they were on the island and they were able to make a few **10.** ________________ sketches of the castle and the birds. It seemed a very short time before Hector returned for them.

Exercise 2

Rewrite the following sentences, replacing the words in bold with a suitable alternative.

1 The boat tossed about on **rough** seas.

2 Our dog had a **rough** coat which needed lots of brushing.

3 The children have had a **rough** time since their father died.

4 Nora had a very tiring journey and is feeling rather **rough**.

5 Anna's parents are snobs and think that the villagers are all **rough** people.

6 The park attendant spoke a few **rough** words to the children and made them cry.

7 Derek has a sore throat and his voice is very **rough**.

8 These are just **rough** plans—they're going to be finalized by an architect.

9 At a **rough** calculation the job should take about a month.

10 The weather was very **rough** but Rob still took the rowing boat out.

A New Arrival

21

Read the following passage carefully, paying particular attention to the words in bold type.

'I asked you to **call** me this morning,' grumbled John to his mother as he stumbled downstairs. 'I thought that you were already up,' said his mother. 'How on earth did you sleep through the church bells? They'**ve been calling** people to worship for about twenty minutes.' John ignored this and asked, '**Has** anyone **called** me?' John's mother replied that his friends, Jenny and Tom, had phoned about five minutes ago to say that they **would call** at the house in about an hour.' John explained that they were going to talk about the fact that the president of the tennis club **had called** a meeting to point out that membership was dwindling fast. 'I **call** it disgraceful that a village this size can't support a tennis club,' said John. 'It's probably because so many of the young people are studying in the city and you and Jenny are waiting to **be called** to the Bar there.' Just then John heard someone **calling** his mother's name. It was their next-door neighbour who was extremely pregnant. 'Please **will** you **call** a doctor! I think the baby's on its way! And my husband's out.' John rushed to make the call and also contacted the neighbour's husband. Soon the mother-to-be was in hospital with her husband by her side. When John and his parents went to see her and the baby next day, John was very pleased that she and her husband had decided to **call** the baby John.

Know the Meaning

call *verb*

1 *(with reference to a person being awakened.)* **wake, wake** *(someone)* **up, get** *(someone)* **up.**

2 *(of bells, etc: The bells are calling people to church.)* **summon, bid.**

3 *(with reference to a telephone.)* **phone, telephone, ring, give** (someone) **a ring.**

4 *(with reference to a personal visit.)* **visit, pay a visit, stop by, drop in.**

5 *(with reference to a meeting, assembly, etc.)* **convene, assemble.**

6 *(Ken said that he called it outrageous that the children were allowed to misbehave.)* **consider, think, regard as, deem, judge.**

7 *(with reference to the legal profession: Jack is studying law and hopes that he will be called to the bar one day.)* **appoint, select.**

8 *(Someone called my name and I turned round.)* **shout, cry out, call out.**

9 *(with reference to someone who will help: Jim immediately called a doctor when Ellie collapsed.)* **send for, ask for, summon.**

10 *(with reference to a child: Bill and his wife have called the baby Rose.)* **name, christen;** *(with reference to a place, building, book, etc: Bob has called his sandwich bar Nosh.)* **name, entitled, style;** *(May called Bert a fool. Terry called the flat a dump.)* **describe as, pronounce, dub, term, label.**

Exercise 1

Find a suitable word that is similar in meaning to 'call' for each blank.

'I asked you to **1.** ____________________ me this morning,' grumbled John to his mother as he stumbled downstairs. 'I thought that you were already up,' said his mother. 'How on earth did you sleep through the church bells? They've been **2.** ____________________ people to worship for about twenty minutes.' John ignored this and asked, 'Has anyone **3.** ____________________ me?' John's mother replied that his friends, Jenny and Tom, had phoned about five minutes ago to say that they would **4.** ____________________ at the house in about an hour.' John explained that they were going to talk about the fact that the president of the tennis club **5.** ____________________ a meeting to point out that membership was dwindling fast. 'I **6.** ____________________ it disgraceful that a village this size can't support a tennis club,' said John. 'It's probably because so many of the young people are studying in the city and you and Jenny are waiting to **7.** ____________________ to the Bar there.' Just then John heard someone **8.** ____________________ his mother's name. It was their next-door neighbour who was extremely pregnant. 'Please will you **9.** ____________________ a doctor! I think the baby's on its way! And my husband's out.' John rushed to make the call and also contacted the neighbour's husband. Soon the mother-to-be was in hospital with her husband by her side. When John and his parents went to see her and the baby next day, John was very pleased that she and her husband had decided to **10.** ____________________ the baby John.

Exercise 2

Rewrite the following sentences, replacing the words in bold with a suitable alternative.

1 The head **is calling** a meeting of all the teaching staff.

____

2 Not all lawyers **are called** to the Bar.

____

3 I asked the hotel porter to **call** me at 6 a.m.

____

4 Sally suddenly saw Ned and **called** his name.

____

5 It was Sunday and the church bells **were calling** people to prayer.

____

6 When the man collapsed, we **called** an ambulance.

____

7 Henry **called** me and left a message on my answering machine.

____

8 The new parents **have called** the baby Molly.

____

9 My mother was ill and her friend **called**, bringing some beautiful flowers.

____

10 Eric **has called** his book Forgotten Dreams.

____

22 Flooded

Know the Meaning

drop *verb*

1 *(of water)* **drip, trickle.**

2 *(of a water level, river, etc: The water level has dropped considerably.)* **fall, sink, go down, subside, abate.**

3 *(of prices or demand)* **fall, go down, decrease, grow less.**

4 *(with reference to a subject, topic, etc: We should drop the subject of politics if we want to stop Joe and Sara arguing.)* **stop, give up, discontinue, abandon.**

5 *(with reference to workers, etc)* **dismiss, discharge, sack, make** (someone) **redundant, let** (someone) **go, shed.**

6 *(informal) (of a person: Bella worked such long hours that eventually she dropped from lack of sleep.)* **collapse, faint, fell down, become unconscious.**

7 *(with reference to an activity: Pam had to drop what she was doing and call for an ambulance.)* **stop, cease, leave, finish, bring to a halt, discontinue, abandon, finish.**

8 *(with reference to an object)* **let fall, let drop, fail to hold.**

9 *(informal) (with reference to a partner: Tom's girlfriend dropped him and went off with someone else.)* **leave, throw** (someone) **over, jilt, give** (someone) **up, abandon, chuck** *(informal).*

10 *(of an object: The plane dropped from the sky.)* **fall, descend, come down, plummet.**

Read the following passage carefully, paying particular attention to the words in bold type.

It had been raining heavily for several days. Although it had stopped now, water still **dropped** from the trees. The high level of the floodwater **was dropping** rapidly, but a lot of damage had been caused to several houses and the town was cut off. It was only possible to get out by boat and very few people had boats. 'Prices will start **dropping** here after this, you'll see!' said one pessimist, and was immediately told to **drop** that subject for the moment. There was enough to worry about without that. Since quite a few of the workers employed by the local authorities **had been dropped** recently because of lack of money, it was taking a long time to clear up the mess caused by the flood. Volunteers had been working day and night and they were now very tired. One of them **had** just **dropped** from exhaustion and had been taken to hospital. Another volunteer had had to **drop** what she was doing and go and see that her elderly parents were OK. Yet another had caused great annoyance by **dropping** a box of food in the water for food was scarce right then. In fact, her mind was not on the clear-up operation because her boyfriend **had** just **dropped** her and she was feeling miserable. People in general were feeling very dispirited but suddenly a cheer went up. Packages **were dropping** from a plane above and they very probably contained food and essential supplies.

Exercise 1

Find a suitable word that is similar in meaning to 'drop' for each blank.

It had been raining heavily for several days. Although it had stopped now, water still **1.** ____________________ from the trees. The high level of the floodwater **2.** ____________________ rapidly, but a lot of damage had been caused to several houses and the town was cut off. It was only possible to get out by boat and very few people had boats. 'Prices will start **3.** ____________________ here after this, you'll see!' said one pessimist, and was immediately told to **4.** ____________________ that subject for the moment. There was enough to worry about without that. Since quite a few of the workers employed by the local authorities **5.** ____________________ recently because of lack of money, it was taking a long time to clear up the mess caused by the flood. Volunteers had been working day and night and they were now very tired. One of them had just **6.** ____________________ from exhaustion and had been taken to hospital. Another volunteer had had to **7.** ____________________ what she was doing and go and see that her elderly parents were OK. Yet another had caused great annoyance by **8.** ____________________ a box of food in the water for food was scarce right then. In fact, her mind was not on the clear-up operation, because her boyfriend had just **9.** ____________________ her and she was feeling miserable. People in general were feeling very dispirited but suddenly a cheer went up. Packages **10.** ____________________ from a plane above and they very probably contained food and essential supplies.

Exercise 2

Rewrite the following sentences, replacing the words in bold with a suitable alternative.

1 If sales don't improve, the firm will have to **drop** several of its workforce.

____

2 **Drop** what you're doing and get out of the building—there's a fire!

____

3 Water **dropped** from our rain hats.

____

4 Tom yelled when he **dropped** the iron bar on his foot.

____

5 The level of the river **is dropping** in the drought.

____

6 Sue's fiancé **dropped** her just before the wedding and married her best friend.

____

7 When plans were passed for a new airport house prices in the area **dropped**.

____

8 The bird had been shot and **dropped** from the sky.

____

9 The children were told to **drop** the subject of extra pocket money.

____

10 Tina **was** almost **dropping** from sheer tiredness.

____

23

Appreciating a Little Sister

Read the following passage carefully, paying particular attention to the words in bold type.

'Leave my **things** alone!' shouted Carol to her little sister, Nell, who was watching her put on her makeup. 'Don't be so nasty to her!' said her mother. 'She's just a baby and people are more important than **things**!' Carol replied, 'One **thing** is that she moves my makeup around and I can't find it. The other day she used a lipstick on her doll and it was the latest **thing**. I had spent a fortune on it.' Carol's mother then remarked, 'You did **things** like that when you were a child. We all do. Try not to get so angry with her. Patience is an essential **thing** to have when dealing with children.' 'Sorry! I'll try to treat Nell better. I'm going to the local shops for a few **things**. Do you want anything?' Her mother replied, 'See if you can find one of those **things** for freshening air. Someone's been smoking in the living room and it smells dreadful.' When Carol came back from the shops, her mother looked worried. Apparently, Nell's friend, Phil, had been run over. Having a **thing** about dogs, he had run over the street to avoid one. The good thing was that he didn't have any severe injuries. 'That was a terrible **thing** to happen! I'm glad he's not too badly hurt,' said Carol and went to give her little sister a special hug. She was very glad that it wasn't her little sister who had been run over.

Know the Meaning

thing *noun*

1 *(Pam's packing all her things—she's moving house.)* **belongings, possessions, stuff** *(informal)*.

2 *(Their furniture was destroyed in the fire but they were all safe and said that things are of little importance in such a situation.)* **object, article, inanimate object**.

3 *(It's a small thing, but I prefer the window open.)* **point, fact, detail, feature, factor**.

4 *(informal) (The fashion designers were showing the latest thing in evening wear.)* **fashion, style, trend, vogue, craze**.

5 *(Most children do naughty things like that.)* **deed, action, act, feat**.

6 *(Tact is a thing that Jenny lacks.)* **quality, characteristic, feature, trait**.

7 *(I need several things from the supermarket.)* **item, article**.

8 *(Jim's gone to buy one of those things for hanging plant pots from.)* **gadget, device, object**.

9 *(Bob yells when he sees a spider—he has a thing about them.)* **phobia, fear, dislike, aversion to**.

10 *(The wedding was the only pleasant thing that happened this year.)* **event, occurrence, incident**.

Exercise 1

Find a suitable word that is similar in meaning to 'thing' for each blank.

'Leave my **1.** ________________ alone!' shouted Carol to her little sister, Nell, who was watching her put on her makeup. 'Don't be so nasty to her!' said her mother. 'She's just a baby and people are more important than **2.** ________________ !' Carol replied, 'One **3.** ________________ is that she moves my makeup around and I can't find it. The other day she used a lipstick on her doll and it was the latest **4.** ________________ . I had spent a fortune on it.' Carol's mother then remarked, 'You did **5.** ________________ like that when you were a child. We all do. Try not to get so angry with her. Patience is an essential **6.** ________________ to have when dealing with children.' 'Sorry! I'll try to treat Nell better. I'm going to the local shops for a few **7.** ________________ . Do you want anything?' Her mother replied, 'See if you can find one of those **8.** ________________ for freshening air. Someone's been smoking in the living room and it smells dreadful.' When Carol came back from the shops, her mother looked worried. Apparently, Nell's friend, Phil, had been run over. Having a **9.** ________________ about dogs, he had run over the street to avoid one. The good thing was that he didn't have any severe injuries. 'That was a terrible **10.** ________________ to happen! I'm glad he's not too badly hurt,' said Carol and went to give her little sister a special hug. She was very glad that it wasn't her little sister who had been run over.

Exercise 2

Rewrite the following sentences, replacing the words in bold with a suitable alternative.

1 People do foolish **things** when they're in love.

____

2 I bought a few **things** in the market.

____

3 The room in the flat was too small to hold Rita's **things**.

____

4 I'm looking for one of those **things** to put on wine bottles, once they have been opened.

____

5 Sam is very materialistic and put **things** before his family and friends.

____

6 Pete can't go up the tower—he has a **thing** about heights.

____

7 One **thing** that annoys Anna about Brian is his loud laugh.

____

8 The accident at the factory was a terrible **thing**.

____

9 This is the latest **thing** in bridal wear.

____

10 Concentration is one **thing** which Garry lacks—and yet he's very clever.

____

24 An Outside Art Class

Know the Meaning

draw *verb*

1 *(with reference to lots, straws, etc. where choice is involved: We drew lots to see who would do the driving.)* **choose, select, pick.**

2 *(with reference to a picture, etc: The class were asked to draw a picture of a castle.)* **sketch, make a drawing of, paint, portray.**

3 *(with reference to earnings: Sam works very hard, but draws a small salary.)* **receive, obtain, get, earn.**

4 *(with reference to a conclusion: We drew the conclusion that Mary was ill.)* **deduce, infer, come to, reach, arrive at.**

5 *(of an exhibit, performance, etc: The show drew huge audiences.)* **attract, gather, lure, capture the attention of, engage the interest of.**

6 *(with reference to a cart, plough, etc: The horse was drawing a caravan.)* **pull, haul, drag, tow.**

7 *(with reference to water: The cottage had no water supply and we had to draw water from a well in the garden.)* **pull up, haul up, extract.**

8 *(with reference to money: Mike went to the bank to draw money to pay his bills.)* **draw out, withdraw, take out.**

9 *(with reference to curtains: We switched on the lights and drew the curtains.)* **close, shut, pull.**

10 *(The warrior drew his sword from its sheath. The man drew a sheaf of banknotes from his wallet.)* **pull out, extract, withdraw, produce.**

Read the following passage carefully, paying particular attention to the words in bold type.

The art class were excited because some were going out of the school for the day, **having drawn** numbers out of a hat to see who would go. It had been decided that it would do the students good to have some outside subjects to **draw**, but it was felt that a reasonably small group would be quite enough to supervise. One of the art teachers, Mrs Williams, had said rather cynically that she **didn't draw** a high enough salary to escort even one member of her class, let alone the whole lot. 'Presumably we **can draw** the conclusion you're not keen on the idea,' said Mr Jones. 'Not at all,' replied Mrs Williams. 'I think it's an excellent idea if the students behave properly.' The place that had been chosen for the experiment was an old-fashioned farm on the edge of town, which regularly **drew** large numbers of visitors. Visitors could see horses **drawing** ploughs and people in peasant dress **drawing** water from a well in a bucket attached to a rope. At the farm Mr Jones went to the bank machine by the farm office to **draw** some money to pay for the entrance fees. He thought at first that the office was closed because someone **had drawn** the curtains. However, an attendant appeared. Mr Jones **drew** a whistle from his pocket, saying that they had to go back to the bus when he blew it. Despite the misgivings of Mrs Williams, all the students behaved well and drew some excellent sketches.

Exercise 1

Find a suitable word that is similar in meaning to 'draw' for each blank.

The art class were excited because some were going out of the school for the day, **1.** ________________ numbers out of a hat to see who would go. It had been decided that it would do the students good to have some outside subjects to **2.** ________________, but it was felt that a reasonably small group would be quite enough to supervise. One of the art teachers, Mrs Williams, had said rather cynically that she didn't **3.** ________________ a high enough salary to escort even one member of her class, let alone the whole lot. 'Presumably we can **4.** ________________ the conclusion you're not keen on the idea,' said Mr Jones. 'Not at all,' replied Mrs Williams. 'I think it's an excellent idea if the students behave properly.' The place that had been chosen for the experiment was an old-fashioned farm on the edge of town, which regularly **5.** ________________ large numbers of visitors. Visitors could see horses **6.** ________________ ploughs and people in peasant dress **7.** ________________ water from a well in a bucket attached to a rope. At the farm Mr Jones went to the bank machine by the farm office to **8.** ________________ some money to pay for the entrance fees. He thought at first that the office was closed, because someone **9.** ________________ the curtains. However, an attendant appeared. Mr Jones **10.** ________________ a whistle from his pocket, saying that they had to go back to the bus when he blew it. Despite the misgivings of Mrs Williams, all the students behaved well and drew some excellent sketches.

Exercise 2

Rewrite the following sentences, replacing the words in bold with a suitable alternative.

1 The puppet show **drew** large crowds.

2 It is quite hard work **drawing** water in a bucket from a well.

3 We **drew** straws to decide which of us would get the free theatre tickets.

4 I'm going to the bank to **draw** money out to pay for my holiday.

5 The students **were drawing** a vase of flowers.

6 Please **draw** the curtains if you're going to switch on the light.

7 With such good qualifications you should be able to **draw** a substantial salary.

8 The man **drew** a packet of sweets from his pocket.

9 It's difficult not to **draw** the conclusion that Bill is lazy.

10 The pony **was drawing** a small cart.

25

Driving Lessons

Read the following passage carefully, paying particular attention to the words in bold type.

'You can't be serious!' said Jenny to her husband, George, who had just announced that he was going to teach their son to drive. 'This is just the **right** time for me—I've got three weeks holiday to take before the end of next month.' George was quite offended when Jenny suggested that he was not at all the **right** person for the job and that they should employ a professional instructor. She pointed out that her husband and son argued about everything, including politics, one having **right** views and one having left. In order to postpone the lessons a little longer and in the hope that George would change his mind, Jenny said, 'Anyway the car's engine doesn't sound **right**. You should get it repaired. Please don't do it yourself. You made a **right** mess of it last time.' Meanwhile George was ignoring her, pretending to read a car-driving manual. Realizing that it was only a pretence, Jenny said, 'It helps to read it **right** side up.' Just for interest she asked him a few questions from the book. George didn't get any of them **right**. He went on to say that it would be difficult to find an instructor whom they could trust. 'Nonsense, I'm sure a properly qualified instructor can be relied upon to do the **right** thing.' George did take his son out for a drive but was back within minutes, crying, '**Right**! I'm phoning an instructor! I told him to take the **right** lane and he took the left!'

Know the Meaning

right *adjective*

1 *(of a time, etc: Mary applied for a job at the right time—a vacancy had just arisen.)* **suitable, fitting, convenient, opportune, ideal.**

2 *(of a person: It will be difficult to find the right person to act as guardian to the little orphan.)* **suitable, appropriate, fitting, fit, ideal.**

3 *(of a person or their opinions, etc with reference to politics: Jim used to be a socialist but his views seem to be extremely right now.)* **right-wing, conservative.**

4 *(of an object: The washing-machine does not sound right.)* **all right, normal, sound, fine.**

5 *(informal) (It was a minor accident, but Amy made a right drama out of it.)* **complete, utter, absolute, real.**

6 *(of an object with two sides: Please put the table cloth on right side up.)* **front, face, upper.**

7 *(of an answer, solution, etc: Only one of the answers to the five questions was right.)* **correct, accurate.**

8 *(It wasn't right of Jack to take the car without permission.)* **correct, proper, decent, honourable.**

9 *(of a direction: The British drive on the right side of the road.)* **right-hand.**

10 *(used as an interjection indicating agreement: Right! I'll follow those instructions.)* **all right, very well, OK** *(informal).*

Exercise 1

Find a suitable word that is similar in meaning to 'right' for each blank.

'You can't be serious!' said Jenny to her husband, George, who had just announced that he was going to teach their son to drive. 'This is just the **1.** ____________ time for me—I've got three weeks holiday to take before the end of next month.' George was quite offended when Jenny suggested that he was not at all the **2.** ____________ person for the job and that they should employ a professional instructor. She pointed out that her husband and son argued about everything, including politics, one having **3.** ____________ views and one having left. In order to postpone the lessons a little longer and in the hope that George would change his mind, Jenny said, 'Anyway the car's engine doesn't sound **4.** ____________. You should get it repaired. Please don't do it yourself. You made a **5.** ____________ mess of it last time.' Meanwhile George was ignoring her, pretending to read a car-driving manual. Realizing that it was only a pretence, Jenny said, 'It helps to read it **6.** ____________ side up.' Just for interest she asked him a few questions from the book. George didn't get any of them **7.** ____________. He went on to say that it would be difficult to find an instructor whom they could trust. 'Nonsense, I'm sure a properly qualified instructor can be relied upon to do the **8.** ____________ thing.' George did take his son out for a drive but was back within minutes, crying, **9.** '____________! I'm phoning an instructor! I told him to take the **10.** ____________ lane and he took the left!'

Exercise 2

Rewrite the following sentences, replacing the words in bold with a suitable alternative.

1 Jim was a **right** fool to resign without first finding another job.

____

2 You failed to give the **right** answer to any of the questions.

____

3 You've come at the **right** moment—I've just finished work.

____

4 Being rude was not the **right** way to act.

____

5 The **right** person for this post needs a great deal of patience.

____

6 Cars made in the UK have the driving wheel on the **right** side.

____

7 Joan's political views are too **right** for Alex.

____

8 **Right**! We'll do what you want.

____

9 That engine doesn't look **all right** to me.

____

10 Could you place the books **right** side up on the table.

____